高校专门用途英语（ESP）系列教材

FINANCIAL ENGLISH
Viewing Listening and Speaking

金融英语视听说教程

黄志华 编

清华大学出版社
北京

内 容 简 介

本书根据金融学学科特点以及学习者的需求和目标，设计了内容丰富、难度适中、形式多样的听力和口语训练任务。全书共10个单元，每单元围绕一个金融类主题开展视听说活动，逐步引导学习者学习和掌握相关的金融英语表达方式，发展金融英语听、说等技能。本书适用于本科院校大学英语拓展类课程，也可作为金融相关专业的金融英语教材。

版权所有，侵权必究。举报：010-62782989，beiqinquan@tup.tsinghua.edu.cn。

图书在版编目（CIP）数据

金融英语视听说教程/黄志华编 .—北京：清华大学出版社，2023.4
高校专门用途英语（ESP）系列教材
ISBN 978-7-302-47437-1

Ⅰ.①金… Ⅱ.①黄… Ⅲ.①金融-英语-听说教学-高等学校-教材 Ⅳ.①F83

中国版本图书馆 CIP 数据核字（2017）第 130941 号

责任编辑：曹诗悦
封面设计：平　原
责任校对：王凤芝
责任印制：曹婉颖

出版发行：清华大学出版社
网　　址：http://www.tup.com.cn, http://www.wqbook.com
地　　址：北京清华大学学研大厦 A 座　　邮　编：100084
社 总 机：010-83470000　　邮　购：010-62786544
投稿与读者服务：010-62776969, c-service@tup.tsinghua.edu.cn
质量反馈：010-62772015, zhiliang@tup.tsinghua.edu.cn

印 装 者：三河市春园印刷有限公司
经　　销：全国新华书店
开　　本：170mm×230mm　　印　张：8.5　　字　数：173 千字
版　　次：2023 年 4 月第 1 版　　印　次：2023 年 4 月第 1 次印刷
定　　价：39.00 元

产品编号：066613-01

前言

编写背景

根据《大学英语教学指南（2020版）》的最新要求，大学英语教学的主要内容可分为通用英语、专门用途英语和跨文化交际三个部分，由此形成相应的三大类课程。《金融英语视听说教程》针对专门用途英语课程门类设计，理念独到、紧扣时事、特色鲜明。本教材通过丰富的视听与口语训练，将金融财经知识贯穿始终，既有利于提高学生英语听说能力，也有助于学生对金融财经知识的了解与应用。

基于财经类大学背景，编者深入调研大学英语课程教学现状和学生听说能力实际情况，落实分类指导、因材施教的原则，将金融财经知识与英语听说技能结合，使学生巩固所学的金融基础知识，同时发展英语听说技能。教材通过对英语的听力技巧和金融财经知识的讲解，让学生学会听懂金融财经新闻，培养学生综合语言运用能力，提高在商务环境中的实战交际能力。

本教材根据学生的认识规律和学习特点，引导学生正确的学习方式，提高学生的自主学习与合作学习能力。教材鼓励教师采用启发式、体验式教学，运用多样化的教学手段，设计生动灵活的教学活动，提升学生在实际商务语境中听说技巧的运用能力，培养学生的创新精神和实践能力。

教材特点

1. 教学内容注重金融财经听力；
2. 融视、听、说技能于一体，发展学生综合语言能力；
3. 涵盖金融财经热点知识，完善金融财经知识体系；
4. 注意培养创新精神，提高学生的实践运用能力；
5. 促进学生自主学习，倡导混合式学习策略。

单元构成

本教材共 10 个单元，每单元围绕一个主要话题设计视、听、说活动。

单元结构安排如下：

Part 1 Background Information 是对财经知识的介绍，帮助学生了解金融财经知识，并为进一步听懂金融财经听力材料、组织对话做铺垫；Part 2 Listening Skills 为听力技巧讲解，并配有针对性的听力技巧训练。

围绕单元主题的视、听练习。视、听练习的语篇取材于多样化的社会热点、真实的金融财经语境，涵盖多元听力题型训练，旨在培养学生用英语获取信息和处理信息的能力。此外，本部分还加入了四、六级的题型，以加强学生应考能力。

围绕单元主题，通过音视频听力导入，训练学生开口说英语的能力。练习形式分为个人发言、同伴互动、小组讨论三种类型。口语任务类型多样，涉及多种财经类语言素材，介绍多种交际功能及与之对应的语言表达手段，部分单元还提供口语对话的范例，让学生根据所提供的语言背景和所学财经知识，自主开展口头训练。

听说技能综合训练，培养学生用英语发表对金融财经现象和观点的评述，以巩固、扩展所学知识并加以实际运用。

编写团队

西南财经大学外国语学院黄志华为教材主编，负责全书构思设计和统稿，以及第4、第9单元的编写；黄明月负责全书审稿和第1单元的编写；冯灿灿负责编写第3、第5单元；张力月负责编写第6、第7单元；苟姝婷负责编写第8单元；都润萍负责编写第2、第10单元；外籍专家Angie Lyons教授审定全稿。在此对上述人员表示感谢！

本教材应新时代的召唤诞生，期待以全新的面貌为新时代专门用途英语教学贡献力量。因教材为全新编写，难免有不足之处，我们将不断收集反馈建议，希望专家、老师和同学在使用中多提宝贵意见，以使教材不断改进和完善。

编者

2022年6月

Contents

Units	Titles	Listening Skills	Speaking Skills	
One	Financial Crisis	Focusing on Specific Information	Talking About Financial Crisis	Page 1
Two	Youth Unemployment Crisis	Identifying the Purpose of Listening	Asking for and Giving Opinions	Page 13
Three	China's GDP Growth	Recognizing Signal Words	Describing Tables and Graphs	Page 29
Four	The Business World	Listening for Cause and Effect	Expressing Ideas	Page 41
Five	The Business Internet Age	Identifying People's Identities	Showing Likes and Dislikes	Page 53
Six	House Prices	Grasping the Main Idea	Expressing Viewpoints	Page 65
Seven	The RMB and the SDR	Making Inferences	Making Comments	Page 75
Eight	Consumption	Listening for Required Information	Making Persuasions	Page 89
Nine	Stocks and the Stock Market	Predicting the Theme and Related Vocabulary in Pre-listening	Describing the Current Situation in the Stock Market	Page 99
Ten	The Gig Economy	Learning to Use Synonymous Substitutions	Describing Similarities and Differences	Page 113

Unit One
Financial Crisis

After studying this unit, you should be able to:

❶ have a broad idea about the financial crisis;

❷ learn to focus on specific information while listening;

❸ know how to take notes while listening;

❹ talk about the financial crisis.

Part ❶ Background Information

The U.S. subprime mortgage crisis was a nationwide banking emergency that coincided with the U.S. recession from December 2007 to June 2009. It was triggered by a sharp decline in housing prices that led to mortgage delinquencies, foreclosures, and the devaluation of housing-related securities. Declines in housing investment preceded the recession and were followed by reductions in household spending and then in business investment. Spending cuts were more pronounced in areas with a combination of high household debt and larger house price declines.

美国次贷危机是一次全国性的银行业危机，发生于 2007 年 12 月至 2009 年 6 月经济衰退期间。房屋价格大幅下滑导致了抵押贷款拖欠、抵押品赎回权取消和房地产证券贬值，从而诱发了这次危机。住房投资的下降要先于经济衰退，紧接着是家庭支出的减少，随后是商业投资的减少。在家庭债务居高和住房价格大幅下降同时出现的区域，支出减少更为显著。

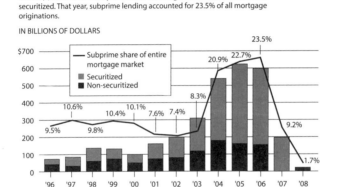

Figure 1　Subprime mortgage originations

① What caused the subprime mortgage crisis?
② In which year was the subprime share of the entire mortgage market at its peak?

Part 2 Listening Skills

Focusing on Specific Information

Understanding the main idea of a listening material is important. However, it is also necessary to focus on specific information. What counts as an important detail depends on the kind of information you want. In general, when listening to a narration of an event, you should pay attention not only to what happened, but also to when, where, how and why it happened. On the other hand, if you are listening to a weather report, the important details are the current weather conditions, the temperature, and the weather forecast.

Task 1 Listen to the recording and fill in the blanks.

1. The _____ in Greece has gained the world's attention. However, some _____ say many other countries are building up dangerous levels of debt.

2. They say _____ are lending money to those countries without enough rules or _____.

3. Greece reached a deal with other European countries to meet its _____ loan _____ last week.

4. Debt activists say there is the _____ of a debt crisis in other areas, especially in the _____. Tim Jones is with a _____ group called the Jubilee Debt Campaign.

5. It studies debt _____ by countries around the world. This month, the group released a report called "The New Debt Trap—How the _____ to the Last Global Crisis Has Laid the Ground for the Next".

6. The Jubilee Debt Campaign says the total amount owed by _____ countries rose 30 percent, from 2011 to 2014, to $13.8 trillion. It _____ that amount will grow to $14.7 trillion this year.

❼ Judith Tyson is with the Overseas Development Institute, a public policy group based in London. She told VOA on Skype that the _____ debt problems are all tied to the _____ of late 2007 and 2008.

❽ While the world financial crisis _____ many countries, some have _____ with debt for 20 years or more. Jamaica, Tim Jones says, is one example.

Note-taking

When listening to long passages, you may want to write down as many details as possible. However, note-taking can be difficult. You may still be writing one sentence while the speaker is five sentences away. By the time you have finished writing, you may not be able to understand what the speaker is saying. In another case, you may consider listening is more important and stop taking notes. By the time you finish listening, you may have already forgotten many important details. In this part, two note-taking skills are introduced.

- Rephrasing sentences for note-taking. Use your own words to describe what you've heard and retain the original meanings.
- Recognizing the main idea. While listening, it is important to select main points or some subordinate points related to the main idea of the listening material.

The following are some discourse markers that can help you recognize the main ideas of listening materials.

I would like to emphasize...

The general point you must remember is...

It is important to note that...

I repeat that...

The next point is crucial to my argument...

Let's move on to another matter...

My next point is...

Another problem to be discussed is...

A related area would be...

Unit One Financial Crisis

Task 2 Listen to the news report and make notes on what you think is important. Then, retell the report based on your notes.

_____

_____

_____

Part 1 Intensive Listening

Word Bank

Shanghai Composite Index a stock market index of all stocks that are traded at the Shanghai Stock Exchange 上海证券综合指数（简称"上证指数"）

brokerage *n.* a company that buys or sells goods or assets for clients 经纪公司

halt *v.* to bring or come to an abrupt stop 停止，终止

household *n.* a house and its occupants regarded as a unit 家庭

Task 1 Listen to the news report and choose the correct answer.

What happened to the Chinese stock market?

A. China's stock markets have lost nearly $3 trillion from their peak in July.

B. The Chinese government hasn't done anything to stabilize the stock market.

C. The Chinese government has introduced a few methods to stop weeks of declining stock prices.

D. By Thursday, the stocks of nearly 1,400 mainland companies have been suspended.

5

Task 2 Listen to the news report. Choose T for true or F for false, and then correct the false statement(s).

1. Major stock indexes, measures that track share values, all had big increases during the month. T F
   _____

2. On June 27th, the Shanghai Composite Index dropped more than eight percent in value, its largest single-day drop in eight years. T F
   _____

3. About 900 companies requested that trading in their shares be halted. T F
   _____

4. The number of households investing in the stock market in China is larger than the number in America. T F
   _____

5. China reported lower economic growth in the past 12 months before June while China's stock market measures gained about 150 percent. T F
   _____

Task 3 Listen to part of the news report again and fill in the blanks.

Companies have also (1) _____ plans to sell new shares on exchanges and, at one point, more than 1,400 companies requested that trading in their shares be (2) _____.

However, China's stock market is not closely (3) _____ to its economy. The Associated Press recently reported a study by the Southwestern University of Finance in Chengdu, China. It said only 8.8 percent of (4) _____ in China are (5) _____ in the market. That is much lower than the 30 percent of households in the U.S. with (6) _____ in the market.

Many of the companies listed on Chinese markets are (7) _____ companies. Investors react to changes in government (8) _____ and to (9) _____ of financing for trading. This can mean that share prices do not follow the economic (10) _____ of the companies that issue them.

Part ❷ Video-watching

Word Bank

credit *n.* If you are given credit, you are allowed to pay for goods or services several weeks or months after you have received them. 赊购

certificate *n.* A certificate is an official document stating that particular facts are true. 证明书

withdraw *v.* to take money out of a bank account (从银行) 取 (钱)

deposit *n.* A deposit is a sum of money which is in a bank account or savings account, especially a sum which will be left there for some time. 存款

mutual *adj.* (of feelings, actions, experience, etc.) shared by two or more people 相互的

Task 1 Watch the video and answer the questions.

❶ What are the choices for Americans to put their money?

_____

_____

❷ How could American savers increase the interest?

_____

_____

❸ What is a money market fund?

_____

_____

Task 2 Watch the video again and fill in the blanks.

① In the United States, people who want to start a _____ have different choices of where to put their money.

② _____ are cooperatives for individuals who often share a work-related connection.

③ With a certificate of deposit, or CD, a person agrees not to _____ the money for a period of time.

④ People have to pay a small _____ to withdraw their money early.

⑤ Money market funds, however, may not be federally _____ like other kinds of saving.

Part 1 Individual Speaking

Word Bank

purchasing power the number of goods or services that can be purchased with a unit of currency 购买力

live off If you live off another person, you rely on them to provide you with money. 靠……生活

on the basis of 根据，鉴于

Unit One Financial Crisis

Task 1 Brainstorm possible changes during the economic crisis.

As we all know, economic crises significantly influence people's lives in many aspects, such as their income, purchasing power, quality of life, bank account, and so on. Now, imagine that you have unfortunately encountered an economic crisis. What will be some of the changes in your life?

Change A: _____

Change B: _____

Change C: _____

Task 2 Watch the video and answer the questions.

① Which event in 2008 changed the previous condition?

_____

_____

② What caused the unemployment in America?

_____

_____

Part ❷ Role-play

A global financial crisis creates a domino effect, meaning that one problem often leads to another. Work in pairs to create an interview about the financial crisis. One acts as a citizen and the other as a policymaker. The following questions may be involved to guide your conversation.

- What causes the financial crisis?
- What will our life be like in a financial crisis?
- What measures can the government take to reduce the influences caused by the financial crisis?

Part 3 Group Work

Tips

Useful expressions for describing influences of the economic crisis

★ The picture shows that...

★ Suffering from...

★ The picture provides miserable experiences...

★ From the table/chart, we can see clearly that... / It is apparent from the chart that...

★ According to the picture...

Task Look at the following pictures and describe the influences resulting from the financial crisis.

Picture 1

Picture 2

Picture 3

Unit One Financial Crisis

Let's Practice

Exercise 1

Task 1 Listen to the news report. Choose T for true or F for false, and then correct the false statement(s).

① Moscow's residents are so worried about the economic crisis that they show no action toward Christmas.   T   F

_____

② According to President Vladimir Putin, the economic contraction will last at least twenty years.   T   F

_____

③ More Russians will be enjoying winter activities this season since they cannot afford to travel abroad.   T   F

_____

④ Maria says that holiday shoppers will be changing their spending habits, and they will no longer buy anything.   T   F

_____

⑤ It's impossible to plunge the country into a full-fledged economic crisis.   T   F

_____

Task 2 Listen to the news report again and fill in the blanks.

　　But a fiscal freeze is (1) _____. Falling oil prices and Western (2) _____ have undermined the ruble, (3) _____ prices for imported goods and pushing Russia toward a (4) _____. President Vladimir Putin says the economic (5) _____ will last a

11

couple of years at most, but that is little (6) _____ to many Russians, including shopper Soso. "I'm trying not to think about it. It's very bad, we'll see how it develops. It's a (7) _____."

♦ Exercise 2

Task Watch the video and answer the questions.

① Which country had the wealthiest citizens in the year 1990?

② Why did the major economic crisis happen in Japan?

Unit Two
Youth Unemployment Crisis

After studying this unit, you should be able to:

① understand the causes of and solutions to the youth unemployment crisis;

② grasp the main idea when listening;

③ identify the purpose of listening;

④ ask for and give opinions on specific topics.

Part ① Background Information

  A total of 357.7 million young people were not in education, employment, or training (NEET) in 2010, and the number is rising. Global Employment Trends for Youth 2015 shows that after rising rapidly between 2007 and 2010, the global youth unemployment rate leveled off at 13 percent between 2012 to 2014; in 2022, according to the Global Employment Trends for Youth, the global youth unemployment rate is currently about 14.9 percent. The number of unemployed youth has increased by 20 million compared to 2016. Thus, we can say that it is still not easy for young people in today's job market.

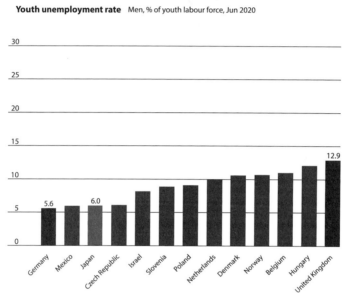

Figure 1   Unemployment rates among various age groups from 2000 to 2014

2010年，未就业、未受教育或未在培训的所谓"尼特族"（NEET）人数达3.577亿，这一数字还在不断增长。国际劳工组织《2015年全球青年就业趋势报告》显示，全球青年的失业率在2007年至2010年之间出现迅猛增长，在2012至2014年之间呈现稳定态势，保持在13%左右的水平。《2022年全球青年就业趋势报告》则显示目前全球青年失业率约为14.9%。青年失业人数相较2016年攀升了2000多万。因此，可以说青年人在当今的劳动力市场仍然举步维艰。

Unit Two Youth Unemployment Crisis

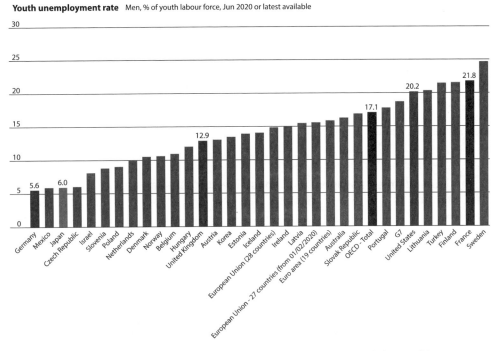

Figure 2   Youth unemployment rate in different regions around the world in 2020

Questions

1. Look at Figure 1 and discuss with your partner why the youth unemployment rate is significantly higher than the adult unemployment rate.
2. Look at Figure 2 and find out which region has the highest or lowest youth unemployment rate.
3. Work in groups to discuss the reasons for the upheaval in youth unemployment.

Part 2 Listening Skills

Identifying Main Ideas

When listening to news reports, lectures, or presentations, it is important to understand the gist or main ideas that the speaker is trying to convey. Here are four keys that can help you identify main ideas as you listen.

First, you should pay special attention to some discourse markers, such as "what I am going to show is...", "the main point is...", etc. The second key is repetition, or how many times a word or phrase is repeated. Third, you should pay attention to the pace, or the speed of the speech. Important points are usually spoken more slowly and clearly. Finally, a speaker's visual aids, such as outlines, lists, and numbers, are obvious clues to the main ideas of the listening material.

Task 1 Listen to the passages and choose the correct answers.

① What does the first passage mainly talk about?
A. The government's labor-market policies have enabled older workers to stay in the labor market longer.
B. Younger workers experienced the biggest relative drop in employment during the recession.
C. The situation and causes of youth unemployment are explained.
D. Attitude and ability are the main reasons that caused youth unemployment.

② What's the main idea of the second passage?
A. The new government of Senegal and governments in neighboring regions face intense pressure to create jobs for young people.
B. The current rate of job creation in Africa will not keep pace with the generation boom.
C. One in two young people who joined rebel movements cite unemployment as their main motivation.
D. Rising youth unemployment endangers Africa's stability.

Task 2 Listen to the passages again and fill in the blanks.

① Younger workers meanwhile experienced the _____ in employment during the recession and have not yet recovered to pre-2008 levels. _____ is still higher than pre-recession levels even though participation for the age group is lower. A recent report found that young people might be held back by a lack of _____ including _____ _____ and that a positive, proactive approach to work was lacking. _____ appear to hinder them more than age.

❷ Africa has the _____ in the world, and _____ are growing. The number of Africans aged 15 to 24 is set to double to 400 million by 2045. The African Development Bank and the UN predict the current rate of job creation, already _____, will not _____ the population boom and this next generation of Africans will struggle to find work. It's a dangerous prospect. The World Bank has found that one in two young people who joined rebel movements cite _____ as their _____. In West Africa, unemployment fuels _____ and recruitment into armed groups, including the Islamist extremist movements in the Sahel.

Identifying the Purpose of Listening

Listening can be the most difficult part of English learning. You may find that after listening to a long passage, you have remembered nothing. Sometimes, even if you force yourself to concentrate on what you are hearing, there are still many distractions that prevent you from properly understanding the material you are listening to. Now here are some listening tips that can be used to help you identify the purpose of the listening material.

- Listen for context.

Let's say your friend says, "I bought this great tuner at JR's. It was really cheap, and now I can finally listen to National Public Radio broadcasts." You don't understand what a tuner is, and focusing on the word "tuner" might frustrate you. This example shows that when you are listening, you need to focus not on the word you don't understand, but on the words you do understand and the whole context.

- Use key words.

Use key words or key phrases to help you understand the general idea. If you understand "New York", "business trip" and "last year", you can assume that the speaker is talking about a business trip to New York last year. Grasping the key words will also help you understand the details.

Task 3 Listen to the passages again and write a summary according to what you have heard.

_____

_____

_____

Task 4 Based on your knowledge and what you just heard, give reasons to support the idea that youth unemployment is a crisis for the whole world.

Part 1 Intensive Listening

Word Bank

International Labor Organization (ILO) a United Nations agency dealing with labor issues, particularly international labor standards, social protection, and work opportunities for all 国际劳工组织

a bleak picture a situation described as pessimistic 一片荒凉的场景

detached *adj.* not attached, separated 分离的

entrenched *adj.* fixed, rooted 确定的

drop out to exclude oneself from the activities; to leave school or an educational program prematurely 离开；退学

marginalized *adj.* to be left to one side 边缘化的

Unit Two Youth Unemployment Crisis

Task 1 Listen to the news report. Choose T for true or F for false, and then correct the false statement(s).

① Young people are facing a big challenge—the lack of jobs. T F

_____

② The economy helps to solve the youth unemployment problem. T F

_____

③ The ILO's report paints a hopeful picture of youth unemployment. T F

_____

④ Few young people are dropping out. T F

_____

Task 2 Listen to the news report again and choose the correct answers.

① What does the news report mainly talk about?
A. The relationship between economy and youth unemployment.
B. The main reason for the youth unemployment crisis.
C. The relationship between labor market and youth unemployment.
D. The current situation of youth unemployment.

② Almost _____ million people between the ages of 15 and 24 are unemployed worldwide, and the ILO's new report predicts no improvement before _____ at the earliest.
A. 65; 2015   B. 70; 2016   C. 75; 2016   D. 75.5; 2017

③ According to the news report, which statement is wrong?
A. Youth unemployment around the world remains at a crisis level.
B. The youth unemployment crisis is becoming entrenched in the market.
C. Neither employed, nor seeking education, many young people are becoming increasingly marginalized.
D. Higher education would surely help young people find a good job.

Task 3 Listen to the news report again and fill in the blanks.

The ILO's report paints a (1) _____ picture of young people losing hope and becoming increasingly (2) _____ from the world of work.

For young people in particular, says the ILO's chief economist Ekkehard Ernst, these years without work will be (3) _____, "We have lost the jobs and they are not coming back. Our forecast shows that we are not getting these jobs back over the next four or five years. So this means that this crisis really becomes (4) _____ on the labor market, and that means that we also see these young people losing their skills."

The ILO already has (5) _____ that many young people are simply (6) _____. Neither in work, nor in education, they have no skills and are becoming increasingly (7) _____. Others are growing (8) _____ that the years spent in higher education have brought no career. Instead, the ILO says, many young graduates are being forced to take part-time (9) _____ jobs.

Part 2 Video-watching

Word Bank

precarious *adj.* unstable, dangerous or difficult and likely to get worse 危险的

graphic *adj.* giving a clear and detailed description 图解的

Tunisia *n.* the northernmost country in Africa 突尼斯

the Arab Spring a revolutionary wave of demonstrations and protests, riots, and civil wars in the Arab world 阿拉伯之春

destabilize *v.* to cause something to be unable to continue existing or working in the usual or desired way 动摇

austerity *n.* a situation in which there is not much money and it is spent only on things that are necessary 紧缩；朴素；节俭

cutback *n.* the act of reducing the number or amount of something 削减

asymmetrical *adj.* not identical on both sides of a central line; unsymmetrical 不对称的

Unit Two Youth Unemployment Crisis

Task 1 Watch the video and answer the questions.

1. In James Heintz's view, what differentiates the growing youth unemployment in developed countries compared to developing countries?

   _____

   _____

2. What are the specific challenges or dangers of working in the informal economy?

   _____

   _____

3. What are the policies that would help young workers integrate into the formal economy and raise their living standards?

   _____

   _____

Task 2 Watch the video again. Write down key words and make an outline. Then, retell the conversation in your own words.

_____

_____

_____

21

Part 1 Individual Speaking

Word Bank

candidate *n.* the prospective recipient of an award or honor, or a person seeking or being considered for some kind of position 候选人

project *v.* to judge or calculate, using the information one has 设想

belie *v.* to be in contradiction with something; to represent falsely 歪曲

hide out to be or go into hiding; to keep out of sight, as for protection and safety 躲藏

endure *v.* to put up with something or somebody unpleasant 忍耐

uprising *n.* organized opposition to authority; a conflict in which one faction tries to wrest control from another 起义

frustration *n.* a feeling of annoyance at being hindered or criticized 挫折

emigrate *v.* to leave one's country of residence for a new one 移居

protest *n.* the act of making a strong public expression of disagreement and disapproval 抗议

detachment *n.* the state of being isolated or detached 分离

Task 1 Brainstorm reasons for unemployment.

When we talk about youth unemployment, we need to find out why people are unemployed. In an ideal labor market, wages would adjust to equilibrate the quantity of labor supplied with the quantity of labor demanded. This wage adjustment would ensure that all workers are always fully employed. But in reality, the unemployment rate never falls to zero. Why does this happen?

Reason A: _____

Reason B: _____

Reason C: _____

Task 2 Watch the video and answer the questions.

① What's the main idea of the video?

_____

_____

② As you know the negative effects caused by the youth unemployment crisis in other countries, talk about the employment challenges faced by Chinese graduates.

_____

_____

Part ❷ Role-Play

Task Work in pairs and conduct a mock interview. One acts as a recruiter from a well-known company and the other as a recent graduate looking for a job at a campus job fair. You can act as you like (sales person, project assistant, advertising planner, etc.). Here are some questions and tips you can use in your interview.

Interview questions:

- What is your biggest weakness?

Tips: The tricky point of this question is that you're being asked about your shortcomings, while your instinct, in an interview situation, is to keep your flaws hidden. What you need to do is to frame your answer so as to give it a positive spin.

Strengths and weaknesses can be different sides of the same coin, so another way to approach this question is to think about how you overcome the potential downside with your greatest strength. For example, if you're a team worker, is it difficult for you to cope with conflict or assume leadership? How do you cope with this?

- Who is your ideal employer?

Tips: Instead of dropping a company name or describing a boss, share the ideal working relationship. For instance, you could say that you would love to work with a manager who is upfront and honest when pointing out mistakes and achievements. Also, you could say that you want to work in a team that tells you exactly what you have to do to get a promotion or salary raise.

- Why do you think you will be appropriate for this job?

Tips: This isn't an invitation to boast, you are being asked to match your abilities to the job. Don't forget it's a very specific question. Why are you suited to this job, as opposed to any other? Thorough employer research before the interview will help you make it.

- How do you manage your time?

Tips: When an employer asks how you manage your time, don't just give an example of how you once finish a task successfully. Your interviewer wants to know your tactics and strategies for getting yourself organized, so you should be ready to describe the approaches you use.

Other questions:

- What has been your greatest achievement?
- Why did you choose your school and course?
- Tell us a situation wherein you led a team.
- Discuss a previous situation wherein you had successfully solved a problem.

Part ❸ Group Work

Useful expressions for asking for opinions

* Do you agree? / Do you agree that...? / Do you think it's a good idea? / Do you think so? / Is this all right with you?
* You don't disagree, do you? / What's your opinion?
* What do you think (about...)? / What are your ideas?
* Do you have any thoughts on that?
* How do you feel about that?

Useful expressions for giving an opinion

* In my opinion/view...
* Generally speaking, I think...
* Personally, I haven't the faintest idea about/whether...
* To my mind...
* I'd just like to say...
* As far as I'm concerned... / As far as I can tell...
* I'm quite convinced that... (Only use this expression to express a very strong opinion!)
* To be quite honest/frank...
* If you ask me..., I'd say that...
* It appears/seems to me... / Let me tell you... / It's quite obvious/clear that...
* I'm pretty/quite/fairly/sure/certain that...

Task Discuss in a group of four and find out some solutions to the youth unemployment crisis. One example is listed below.

Q: What's your opinion on easing the problem of youth unemployment?
A: As far as I'm concerned, more attention should be paid to providing youth with skills, qualifications and vocational pathways that will lead directly to employment opportunities.

Exercises

Task 1 Watch the video and fill in the blanks.

We need to move (1) _____ to tackle the crisis of youth unemployment.

The official figures say that (2) _____ million of them are unemployed, and that's not even calculating all the young people who have stopped looking for work or are (3) _____. The number is actually much larger.

A quarter of a billion young people who are not in school or in work are underemployed, so that's a large portion of the (4) _____ billion young people who are under the age of (5) _____. If we can reduce youth unemployment by (6) _____, that may result in 72 billion dollars in new revenue. This is something that companies and governments should care about. We need to invest in the future, and young people are future consumers and taxpayers.

The skills gap

It's counterintuitive that as we have a global crisis in youth unemployment, we have jobs that are going (7) _____, because businesses say they can't find the (8) _____ that they need. There are young people coming out of high school or university with qualifications, but with no meaningful skills that businesses want.

At Education for Employment, we've shown that it works to switch the process to start on the demand side, to start with the market. We ask what the jobs that are needed and what the sectors of growth are. We talk to businesses to understand the skill needs, and then we design programs to meet those needs. All of our employers say what's needed most are (9) _____, (10) _____, and (11) _____. The emphasis has to be on non-cognitive, entrepreneurial and creative skills—those basic soft skills that will allow a young person to be successful no matter what industry they're in.

There are things that we can do to create internship and apprenticeship programs that (12) _____ school and work. These are the things that are already being done, and now need to be scaled up.

The information gap

There are some young people. All they need is (13) _____. So we've developed a program called "Finding a job as job". It's three days. It's delivered in universities and (14) _____ and just teaches young people the basics about how to go after jobs, how to do that job search, and where the jobs are. That's the information gap and it can be easily filled.

Task 2 Watch the video again. Choose T for true or F for false, and then correct the false statement(s).

1. If we get young people involved in lots of entrepreneur activities, entrepreneurship may give them opportunities to potentially launch a new business.   T   F

   _____

2. Setting up small businesses is proving to be meaningless in motivating the creative potential of young people.   T   F

   _____

3. The large companies are the engines of growth and the job creators in many markets.   T   F

   _____

4. The talent pipeline should be created for the young people, and they themselves should understand what kind of skills will contribute to their job growth.   T   F

   _____

❺ We need to help young people understand that joining a small company can be just as rewarding.　　　　　　　　　　　　　　　T　　　F

Task 3 Watch the video again and retell the main ideas of the speaker. Give your own ideas about youth unemployment and share them with your classmates.

Unit Three
China's GDP Growth

After studying this unit, you should be able to:

❶ understand the general trend of China's GDP growth;

❷ recognize signal words while listening;

❸ know how to improve short-term memory;

❹ explain the factors influencing GDP growth and describe the state of GDP growth in tables and graphs.

Part ❶ Background Information

GDP (Gross Domestic Product) is the market value of all final goods and services produced in a country during a given period. It is commonly used to measure the economic performance of an entire country or region and can also measure the relative contribution of an industry sector. The more common use of GDP is to calculate the growth of the economy from year to year (and more recently from quarter to quarter). The pattern of GDP growth is used to indicate the success or failure of economic policy and to determine whether an economy is "in recession".

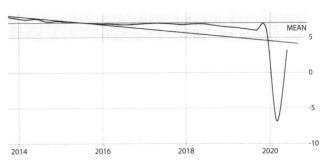

Source: tradingeconomics.com | National Bureau of Statistics of China

For the last 40 years or so, China has enjoyed high economic growth since the reform and opening-up policy. However, China is encountering many problems concerning its economic development, such as transforming the economic growth pattern, adjusting the industrial structure, and reforming the financial system. But it is believed that persistent and gradual policy reforms and institutional changes will reduce distortions, improve economic incentives and further promote China's rapid economic growth in the future.

国内生产总值（GDP）指在某一既定时期一国生产的所有最终产品与服务的市场价值。GDP通常用于衡量一个国家或地区的经济发展状况，同时也可用于衡量一个行业领域的相对贡献。GDP更是计算每年或每季度的经济增长状况常用的衡量标准。其增长模式预示着经济政策实施的成败，也决定着经济是否处于"衰退期"。

改革开放40多年来，中国经济呈快速发展的态势。但是，中国的经济发展也遇到了许多问题，如转变经济增长模式、调整产业结构以及改革金融体系等。但是，我们相信持久且渐进的政策改革和制度转变将减少经济发展的畸形态势，完善经济发展的激励措施，进而促进未来中国经济的快速增长。

Questions

❶ What does GDP stand for? Why is GDP so important?

❷ What are the current problems in China's economy?

❸ Look at the graph above and discuss with your partner: What's the trend in China's GDP growth? What possible reasons can you think of to explain this trend?

Part 2 Listening Skills

Recognizing Signal Words

Signal words serve as signposts guiding you through all the information you hear. If you catch these words, it would be easier for you to understand the main point. The following are different types of signal words.

- Contrast signal words: *although, but, despite, however, in contrast*, etc.
- Cause and effect signal words: *because, so, therefore, accordingly, consequently, as a result*, etc.
- Support signal words: *and, or, also, additionally*, etc.
- Sequence/order signal words: *first(ly), second(ly), finally, then, before, after*, etc.
- Example signal words: *for example, such as, like, in other words*, etc.
- Emphasis signal words: *actually, I mean, namely, that is to say*, etc.
- Conclusion signal words: *in conclusion, in summary, hence*, etc.

Task 1 Listen to the recording and fill in the blanks.

It is logical to suppose that things (1) _____ good labor relations, good working conditions, good wages and benefits, (2) _____ job security motivate workers. (3) _____ one expert, Frederick Herzberg, argued that such conditions do not motivate workers; they are merely satisfiers.

Motivators, (4) _____, include things (5) _____ having a challenging and interesting job, recognition and responsibility. (6) _____, even with the development of computers and robotics, there are always plenty of boring, repetitive and mechanical jobs, and lots of unskilled people who have to do them. (7) _____ how do managers motivate people in such jobs?

One solution is to give them some responsibilities, (8) _____ as individuals, (9) _____ as part of a team. (10) _____, some supermarkets combine office staff, the people who fill the shelves, and the people who work at the checkout into a team. And let them decide what product lines to stock, how to display them, and so on.

Task 2 Classify the signal words you have filled in Task 1.

_____

_____

_____

Improving Short-term Memory

There are two kinds of memory: short-term memory and long-term memory. Information in long-term memory can be recalled at a later time when it is needed. The information may be kept for days or weeks. In contrast, information in short-term memory is kept for only a few seconds. The following are some tips for you to improve your short-term memory.

- Retell the original text at once.

You can improve your short-term memory by repeating the information over and over. Once the speaker stops, retell the whole text immediately. It doesn't matter if you can't use the original expressions. Using your own words can also be helpful.

- Grasp the details when listening for the first time.

In short-term memory practice, you are also supposed to concentrate on the important words, like numbers and verbs, and repeat them after the listening practices.

Task 3 Listen to the passage and take notes on key words and phrases.

_____

_____

_____

Unit Three China's GDP Growth

Task 4 Listen to the passage again and repeat the main idea based on the expressions given below. You may refer to the notes you have written down in Task 3.

In the next few decades, ...

So after a few years, ...

Some of the large automobiles are...

Transportation in the future...

In the future, ...

Task 5 Listen to the passage again and choose the correct answers.

1. What will be used to power cars in the next few decades?
   A. Synthetic fuel. B. Solar energy.
   C. Gas. D. Electricity.

2. What will future news reports focus on when we talk about transportation?
   A. Air traffic conditions. B. Traffic jams on highways.
   C. Road conditions. D. New traffic rules.

3. What will passengers be probably asked to do when they travel to the moon?
   A. Go through a health check. B. Carry little luggage.
   C. Arrive early for boarding. D. Undergo security checks.

 Listen

Part 1 Intensive Listening

Word Bank

poverty *n.* the state of having little or no money or no material possessions 贫穷

sanitation *n.* the state of being clean and conductive to health 卫生环境

potentially *adv.* with a possibility of becoming actual 潜在地

address *v.* to deal with verbally or in some form of artistic form 处理

diminish *v.* to decrease in size, extent, or range 减少

Task 1 Listen to the passage and choose the correct answers.

1. Which country has emerged in recent times as a big spender in the international market?
   A. Nigeria.　　　B. China.　　　C. Japan.　　　D. The UK.

2. The country has about _____ of its population living on less than 1 dollar per day.
   A. one third　　B. two thirds　　C. three fourths　　D. one and a half

Task 2 Listen to the dialogue. Choose T for true or F for false, and then correct the false statement(s).

1. The latest report shows China's economic development has slowed to 4% in a third quarter of 2019 year-on-year.　　　　　　　　　　　　　　T　　F

___

2. The economic development in 2019 is the slowest in almost three decades.
   　　　　　　　　　　　　　　　　　　　　　　　　　　　T　　F

Unit Three China's GDP Growth

❸ The Chinese authorities say the economic development remained stable only despite the domestic challenges. T F

___

❹ The economic performance is not in line with the Chinese government projections of GDP growth between 6 and 6.5%. T F

___

Task 3 Listen to the passage and choose the correct answers.

❶ What does the passage mainly talk about?
A. To explain what extreme poverty is.
B. To show the progress that has been made in dealing with poverty.
C. To discuss how to tackle poverty.
D. To tell us that poverty is our enemy.

❷ What condition further complicates the goal of eradicating poverty?
A. Economic slowdown in developed and emerging economies.
B. The large amount of poor people.
C. A lack of basic human needs.
D. Poor infrastructure.

❸ BRICS countries include _____.
A. Brazil, Russia, India, China and South Africa.
B. Britain, Russia, India, China and South Korea.
C. Brazil, Russia, India, China and South Korea.
D. Britain, Russia, India, China and South Africa.

Task 4 Listen to the passage again and fill in the blanks.

What is extreme poverty? According to (1) _____, it's a condition characterized by a lack of basic human needs, like (2) _____ drinking water, food, sanitation and

35

(3) _____.

The good news, says World Bank president Jim Yong Kim, is that the world has made some progress. "Over (4) _____, we've gone from nearly two billion people living in extreme poverty to fewer than one billion." Despite inroads, nearly a billion people still live on less than (5) _____ per day.

One (6) _____ is to partner with new (7) _____ institutions such as the Asian Infrastructure and Investment Bank led by China and the New Development Bank (8) _____ by the so-called BRICS countries.

"We at the World Bank Group see these development banks as (9) _____ very strong (10) _____ in tackling the enormous challenge of bringing much needed infrastructure to the developing world."

Part 2 Video-watching

Task Watch the video and answer the questions.

1. Whom will the G7 increase their global aid for?

2. What does G7 say about Brexit?

Unit Three China's GDP Growth

Let's Speak

Part 1 Individual Speaking

Task 1 Brainstorm factors promoting the economic growth.

What factors can promote the economic growth?

Factor A: _____

Factor B: _____

Factor C: _____

Task 2 Watch the video and answer the questions.

❶ Why did China avoid rolling out trillion-dollar stimulus packages like the US and Japan?

_____

_____

❷ Why are consumers curbing their spending?

_____

_____

Part 2 Role-play

Task 1 China's GDP generally keeps growing. In our daily life, we all benefit from the GDP growth. Now discuss with your partner what benefits you can get from the GDP growth.

Task 2 Work in pairs. One acts as the parent and the other as the son/daughter. Talk about our changes of life in different aspects, and try to explore whether these changes are brought about by the GDP growth.

Unit Three China's GDP Growth

 Part ③ Group Work

Tips

Useful expressions for describing trends of graphs

* This chart shows the changes in the number of… over the period from… to…
* The chart illustrates that…
* The graph provides some data regarding…
* The diagram shows that…
* The graph depicts that…
* The figures/statistics show that…
* The diagram reveals how…

* The data lead us to the conclusion that…
* The number sharply went up to…
* The figure peaked at…
* … decreased year by year…
* The figures bottomed out in…
* There is an upward trend in the number of…
* Form… to…, the rate of decrease slows down.

Task Look at the graph below. Work in groups to discuss and describe the GDP trend from 2020 to 2022. Then give a report about your group findings.

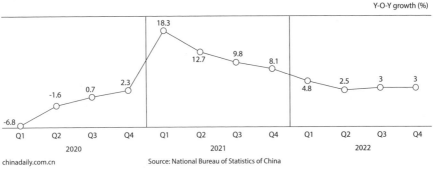

Trend of GDP Growth — Y-O-Y growth (%)

chinadaily.com.cn   Source: National Bureau of Statistics of China

Exercises

Task Watch the video and answer the questions.

① If we want to compare our economy over time, what should we do?

② How much did the population grow between 1950 and 2015 in the US?

Unit Four
The Business World

After studying this unit, you should be able to:

① understand the types of businesses and the different departments in the business;

② identify logical relationships within the passage;

③ identify main events while listening;

④ understand how the macro-economy affects business in a country.

 Learn

Part ① Background Information

A business is a legally recognized organization designed to provide goods or services to consumers. Businesses predominate in economies, most being privately owned and formed to make a profit that will increase the wealth of their owners and grow the business itself. A business can be a for-profit entity, such as a publicly-traded corporation, or a non-profit organization engaged in business activities. Notable exceptions include cooperative enterprises and state-owned enterprises. Enterprises may also be non-profit or state-owned.

企业是被法律认可的组织，旨在为顾客提供商品与服务。企业在经济中占有主导地位，其中大部分为私有企业，以增加自身财富与扩大企业规模为目的来获取盈利。企业可以是以盈利为目的的实体，如上市公司，也可是参与企业活动的非营利组织。当然，合作企业和国有企业明显不包括在内。此外，企业可以分为非营利形式或国有形式。

Questions

1. What are businesses?
2. What products do you usually use from companies and why do you like them?
3. What characteristics can help a business to be successful?

Part 2 Listening Skills

Listening for Cause and Effect

The easiest way to define cause and effect is "one thing leads to another". The one thing is the cause that leads to (or results in) "another". While listening, you should pay special attention to words which show the reason, such as "because, due to, since, for, as, owing to", etc. Besides, some phrases, such as "result from, derive from" and "attribute to", also have this function. Also, some non-finite verbs can represent the cause and effect, for example, "Failing the exam, she cried." If you recognize these words and understand the cause and effect of the event, you will know the logical relationships within the whole event.

Unit Four The Business World

Task 1 Listen to the news report and answer the questions.

1. What is important for economic growth in Africa?
   _____
   _____

2. What is the main problem facing African universities?
   _____
   _____

3. Why do African universities receive less funding?
   _____
   _____

Task 2 Listen to the news report again and fill in the blanks.

1. African universities face a number of issues, including _____
   _____.

2. According to engineering professor David Mfinanga, African universities should balance _____ and _____.

3. Although African universities struggle for funding, they cannot solve this problem right now because _____.

4. Another serious problem is that there are many university graduates but few _____
   _____.

5. Solving higher education's problems may help solve other problems like _____
   _____.

43

Identifying Main Events

Sometimes you cannot remember all the details of what you have heard, so you need to identify the most important events. There are some methods to make sure which part is the most important one. First, the main event is usually mentioned at the beginning or the end of a passage. Second, the main event is usually repeated more than once within a passage. Third, pay attention to the logic of the passage, such as causal relationship, coordinating relationship, and adversative relationship, which will help you remember more details of the main event.

Task 3 Listen to the passage and answer the questions.

① What is a proprietor?

② What does partnership mean?

③ How long does the partnership exist?

④ What would happen if the shares lost value?

⑤ What is an entity?

Unit Four The Business World

Task 4 Listen to the passage again and fill in the blanks.

Types of business	Explanations
(1) _____	The owner and the company are the same. This means the proprietor gets to keep all of the profits of the business, but must also pay any debts.
Partnership	(2) _____
(3) _____	These have full partners and limited partners. Limited partners may not share as much in the profits, but they also have less responsibility for the business.
Corporation	(4) _____
Non-profit groups	(5) _____

Part 1 Intensive Listening

Word Bank

turn sb. down to refuse an offer, a job, or a request 拒绝

pull out all the stops to do everything possible in order to do or achieve something 全力以赴

keep control of to assume a position of power over a person, group, or thing 控制

live with to put up with something 忍受

45

Task 1 Listen to the recording and answer the questions.

1. When did the speaker set up the company?

   _____

   _____

2. What kind of company is it?

   _____

   _____

3. What is the main problem of the company?

   _____

   _____

4. What efforts did they make?

   _____

   _____

5. What technology has made them successful?

   _____

   _____

Task 2 Listen to the recording and answer the questions.

1. What does it take to be a good department store buyer?

   _____

   _____

2. What does Karen's job involve?

   _____

   _____

❸ Why does Karen think she has got the best job?

_____

_____

Task 3 Listen to the recording and choose the correct answers.

❶ Why can't human beings prevent the world from being polluted?

A. Because we want the benefits.

B. Because we use too many chemical materials.

C. Because we have less industry.

D. Because we plant more trees.

❷ According to the speaker, which of the following do people value most?

A. Industrial development.

B. Their own health.

C. Their children's future.

D. Sound environment.

❸ What does the story about the pilot indicate?

A. Man knows where the society is going.

B. The speaker is worried about the future of our modern society.

C. People don't welcome the rapid development of modern society.

D. Man can do nothing about the problem of pollution.

Task 4 Listen to the dialogue. Choose T for true or F for false, and then correct the false statement(s).

❶ The biggest toy store initially turned me down, so I lost the opportunity.　T　　F

_____

❷ I tried my best to prepare the presentation.　　　　　　　T　　F

___

❸ I sold one million pounds worth of toys in the first year.　　T　　F

___

❹ Ten percent of my business is worth ten million pounds.　　T　　F

___

❺ You have to be decisive and accept the consequences of what you have done.

　　　　　　　　　　　　　　　　　　　　　　　　　　　T　　F

___

Task 5 Listen to the dialogue again and fill in the blanks.

A: At first, no. The biggest toy store (1) _____ turned me down, but finally I saw their (2) _____, Jim Taylor. He liked my business plan, but told me that what I had to offer probably had (3) _____ to him. So I asked for five minutes to do a presentation and I pulled out all the stops. I made a Ferris wheel, a windmill and a bulldozer and within (4) _____, Jim Taylor was won over. I sold one million pounds worth of toys through his store that first year.

B: (5) _____. But it didn't stop there, did it?

A: No. Elto, one of the companies which had turned me down initially, (6) _____ me and said they were interested in my designs after all. So I (7) _____ a deal with them to (8) _____ to make Klikset and market it abroad. I even persuaded them to buy ten percent of my business for ten million pounds. They wanted a (9) _____ but I wanted to keep control of my business.

B: Finally, Desmond, what do you put your success down to?

A: Well, however much you plan, you can never be sure how things will turn out. You have to make decisions and just live with the (10) _____. I've always learnt something from my mistakes.

B: Well, thank you Desmond for your wonderful...

Unit Four The Business World

Part 2 Video-watching

Word Bank

cash flow the movement of money into and out of a business as goods are bought and sold 现金流

vendor *n.* a company or person offering something for sale, especially a trader in the street 卖主

entrepreneurial spirit an idea and a culture that entrepreneurs strive for 企业家精神

Task 1 Watch the video and answer the questions.

1. What are the biggest costs and risks cited by small business owners?

   _____
   _____

2. What is the current condition of small businesses in the US?

   _____
   _____

3. What is the main idea of the video?

   _____
   _____

Task 2 Watch the video again. Take notes and make an outline. Then, retell it.

   _____
   _____
   _____

Speak

Part ❶ Individual Speaking

Task 1 Brainstorm marketing campaign strategies.

If you were a marketer in a company, how would you run a successful marketing campaign to sell your products?

Strategy A: _____

Strategy B: _____

Strategy C: _____

Task 2 Read the following passage and answer the questions.

Actually, marketing is arguably the most important aspect of management. You can manage your materials and production processes well, but if no one buys your products, your business will fail. Marketing is not just about advertising. It is all the processes involved in supplying customers with the right products at the right time and at the right price.

So, how does one conduct a successful marketing campaign? First, the marketer should be clear about the needs of current and potential customers. The starting point is to fully explore where the customer lives. What are the basic motivations behind their purchasing decisions? A marketer should assess the market, including competitors, distributors, technology, and social trends. Third, the company should have creative ideas, both for products and services. In this way, the idea and its elements become the brand. The brand stands out because its positive differences from the competition are clear.

❶ In the passage, what are the three steps in a successful marketing campaign?

_____

_____

2 Which step do you think is the most important one? Why?

_____

_____

Part 2 Role-play

Tips

> **Useful expressions for bargaining over the price**
>
> **Customer**
>
> ★ That's unreasonable! I'd take it for $10.
> ★ This is out of my price range!
> ★ Lower the price, and I'll consider it.
> ★ Could you give this for cheaper?
> ★ How about buy one and give one free?
>
> **Salesman**
>
> ★ I'm afraid I can't drop the price any more.
> ★ Sorry, but my offer is based on a minimal profit.
> ★ What's your general price range?
> ★ I'm not kidding, but we are making a fair deal.
> ★ I'm afraid I can't agree with you. I have to make a living!

Task Suppose you go to a store to buy a T-shirt. A yellow T-shirt looks quite good on you, but the price is pretty high. You want to bargain over the price. Work with your partner. One acts as the customer and the other as the salesman or saleswoman.

Part 3 Group Work

Task You are part of a team of talented and creative young people who want to start a business now. But there are a lot of things to think about first. Work in groups of four. Think of a creative or interesting idea to support your business and make it feasible. Use what you have learned in this unit to perfect your idea. The following questions may help you. Then give a group presentation to your class.

- What types of companies do you prefer?
- What products do you want to sell?
- Who are your target consumers?
- What makes your products different from others?
- How could you attract customers?

Let's Practice

Exercises

Task 1 Watch the video and discuss who would benefit if the value of the Russian ruble depreciates. List the reasons.

_____
_____
_____

Task 2 The development of businesses is closely linked to the economic situation of their country. Write down other external factors that affect businesses.

_____
_____
_____

Unit Five
The Business Internet Age

After studying this unit, you should be able to:

❶ understand the two main applications of the Internet: social networking and e-commerce;

❷ identify people's identities while listening;

❸ recognize commonly used currency units;

❹ know how to express likes and dislikes in business settings.

Let's Learn

Part ❶ Background Information

    The Internet has been in widespread use since the 1980s. In the 25 years since 1995, the number of users has increased 100-fold, reaching more than a third of the world's population. The entertainment and consumer industries are perhaps the fastest growing segments of the Internet. The Internet has enabled and accelerated new forms of personal interactions through instant messaging, Internet forums, and social networking. Online shopping has grown exponentially for both retailers and traders. Now most of us can not live without the Internet. We are living in the Internet age.

从20世纪80年代开始，互联网得到了广泛应用。在1995年之后的25年里，互联网用户已经增长了百倍，超过世界人口总数的三分之一。娱乐业和消费业的互联网发展大概是最为迅速的。互联网通过即时通信、网络论坛和社交网络，促进和加速了人际互动新形式的形成和发展，主要零售业和贸易行业的网络购物均呈指数级增长。如今，大部分人已离不开互联网。我们正生活在互联网时代。

Questions

❶ How much do you know about the Internet?

❷ What benefits can you get from the Internet?

❸ Do you think we are living in the Internet age? Why?

Part 2 Listening Skills

Identifying People's Identities

Identity is a person's conception and expression of his/her own and others' individuality or group membership. Identifying people's identities is always the first step in communication or interaction. Here are some categories of people's basic identities.

- Gender identity: man/male, woman/female.
- Age identity: youth, teenager, adult, middle-aged people, old people, etc.
- Marital identity: unmarried/single, married/non-single, etc.
- Educational identity: primary school student, junior high school student, senior high school student, bachelor, master, doctor, etc.
- Professional identity: professor, doctor, policeman, worker, businessman, accountant, banker, investor, etc.

Task 1 Listen to the dialogues and choose the correct answers.

1. Who is the woman?
   A. A nurse.   B. A bride.   C. A hostess.   D. A waitress.

2. Who is the woman most likely to be?
   A. A teacher.   B. A principal.   C. A mother.   D. A doctor.

3. Who is the man?
   A. A driving instructor.   B. A government official.
   C. A parent.   D. A policeman.

4. Who is the woman most likely to be?
   A. A professor.   B. A cleaning woman.
   C. A friend.   D. A fellow student.

5. Who is the woman most likely to be?
   A. A housekeeper.   B. An electrician.
   C. A construction worker.   D. A house guest.

Task 2 Listen to the passage and fill in the blanks.

W: I'm Shirley Griffith.

M: And I'm Steve Ember with the VOA Special English program *People in America*. Every week we tell about a person who was important in the history of the United States. Today, we tell about Anne Morrow Lindbergh. She was a famous (1) _____ and (2) _____.

W: Anne Morrow Lindbergh was the (3) _____ of the famous pilot, Charles Lindbergh. She flew aeroplanes with him as his (4) _____. She wrote more than ten books of memories, fiction, poetry and essays. Critics had called her books "small works of (5) _____". Anne Spencer Morrow was born in (6) _____ in Englewood, New Jersey. Her father was a very rich (7) _____. He later became the American (8) _____ to Mexico. Her mother was an (9) _____ and (10) _____. Anne went to Smith College in Northampton, Massachusetts. She wanted to become a writer. She won two major prizes from the college for her writing.

Recognizing Currency Units

Different countries use different currency units, and currencies with different units may represent different values even when they are in the same number. As a medium of exchange, currency plays an active role in the international trade. The following are some commonly used currency units.

Currency unit	Full name	Currency symbol	Name in Chinese
CNY	Chinese Yuan	¥	人民币
USD	United States Dollar	$	美元

Continued

Currency unit	Full name	Currency symbol	Name in Chinese
EUR	Euro	€	欧元
JPY	Japanese Yen	¥	日元

Task 3 Listen to the recording about the currency units and methods of payment. Write down what you have heard.

_____ _____ _____ _____

_____ _____ _____ _____

_____ _____ _____ _____

_____ _____ _____

Task 4 Listen to the dialogues and choose the correct answers.

❶ What kind of currency does the woman have?
   A. RMB.   B. USD.   C. GBP.   D. JPY.

❷ Which one doesn't the woman want?
   A. 10.   B. 15.   C. 20.   D. 25.

❸ (1) What kind of currency does the woman want?
   A. RMB.   B. USD.   C. GBP.   D. JPY.

   (2) How much can the woman exchange?
   A. 2,000 RMB.   B. 2,000 USD.   C. 2,000 GBP.   D. 2,000 JPY.

❹ (1) What kind of currency does the woman want?
   A. RMB.   B. USD.   C. GBP.   D. JPY.

(2) How much does the woman want to exchange?

A. 3,000 RMB.   B. 3,000 USD.   C. 3,000 GBP.   D. 3,000 JPY.

❺ What kind of currency will the woman have?

A. RMB.   B. USD.   C. GBP.   D. JPY.

❻ What kind of currency can't the man exchange?

A. USD.   B. Japanese Yen.   C. Hong Kong dollar.   D. GBP.

Part 1 Intensive Listening

Word Bank

online shopping consumers directly buy goods or services from a seller over the Internet 网购

e-commerce electronic commerce, which is the trading of products or services using computer networks, such as the Internet 电子商务

Singles' Day a day for unmarried or uncoupled people to celebrate their lives on November 11 光棍节

Thanksgiving Day a national holiday celebrated in Canada and the United States as a day of giving thanks for the blessing of the harvest and of the preceding year on the last Thursday of November 感恩节

blockbuster *n.* something that is very successful, especially a very successful book or film 轰动，一鸣惊人的书（或电影）

Unit Five The Business Internet Age

Task 1 Listen to the passage and choose the correct answers.

① What does the passage mainly talk about?
A. Singles' Day.
B. Alibaba.
C. A retail blockbuster.
D. Online shopping day.

② What's the biggest online shopping day in the world?
A. Cyber Monday.
B. China's Singles' Day.
C. Black Friday.
D. Thanksgiving Day.

③ When did China's Singles' Day become a shopping day?
A. 2008.   B. 2009.   C. 2010.   D. 2011.

Task 2 Listen to the passage again and fill in the blanks.

Not Valentine's Day. Not Cyber Monday or Black Friday. They are the days that follow Thanksgiving in the U.S. and usher in the start of the holiday shopping season. The winner is China's (1) _____, celebrated (2) _____.

It became a major shopping day in (3) _____. The CEO of an online shopping site—(4) _____—sought to increase sales at the (5) _____ company. The CEO, Daniel Zhang, launched an annual online sale that day, said *Fortune*.

Last year, Alibaba sold more than (6) _____ worth of products in the (7) _____ of the sales, reported Bloomberg. Total sales on Singles' Day soared to (8) _____ within 24 hours. That's four times bigger than Cyber Monday in the U.S., which is the Monday after Thanksgiving and traditionally a big shopping day. By comparison, online sales in the U.S. last year on Black Friday were just (9) _____, reported TechCrunch.

Today, Singles' Day is a (10) _____ blockbuster. Analysts predict that this year, sales on China's Singles' Day will soar to a new high.

Part 2 Video-watching

Word Bank

virtual *adj.* a virtual (rather than actual) version of something 虚拟的

bug *n.* a software bug which is an error, flaw, failure, or fault in a computer program or system that causes it to produce an incorrect or unexpected result, or to behave in unintended ways 故障

time-sharing the sharing of a computing resource among many users by means of multi-programming and multi-tasking 分时

the military/commercial/scientific network the computers are connected for special uses, such as the military use, commercial use, scientific use and so on 军事、商业、科技互联网

Task 1 Watch the video and answer the questions.

① When did the "Internet" begin?

② What problems did computer developers encounter before the Internet came up?

③ What is the first concept in computer technology to share the processing power of one computer with multiple users?

④ What are the major fundamental concepts regarding the history of the Internet?

Unit Five The Business Internet Age

Task 2 Watch the video again, and take down the major events in different periods of the history of the Internet with as few words as possible.

In 2009: _____

Before 1957: _____

In 1957: _____

After 1957: _____

Part 1 Individual Speaking

Word Bank

budget *n.* a quantitative expression of a plan for a defined period of time, which may include planned costs and expenses 预算

online review the comments on the Internet 在线评论

coupon *n.* a ticket or document that can be redeemed for a financial discount or rebate when purchasing a product 优惠券

discount *n.* reductions in the basic prices of goods or services 打折

free shipping the goods are delivered to you without paying any fee 免运费

credit card a payment card issued to users (cardholders) as a method of payment 信用卡

Task 1 Brainstorm some tips for shopping online.

What are the top three tips you are most likely to follow when shopping online?

Tip 1: _____

Tip 2: _____

Tip 3: _____

Task 2 Watch the video, and then discuss the questions.

1. Why are the online shopping tips important to us?
2. What are the main online shopping tips mentioned in the video?

Part 2 Role-play

Bargaining is a type of negotiation and transaction in which the buyer and seller discuss the price. If the bargaining results in an agreement on terms, the transaction takes place. Bargaining also takes place when shopping online, for example, bargaining for a discount, a coupon, free shipping and so on.

Task Work in pairs. One acts as the online seller and the other as the online buyer. You can negotiate a pair of shoes or something else with your partner.

Part ❸ Group Work

Tips

Useful expressions for showing likes and dislikes

- ★ I like/love…
- ★ I am fond of / pleased with / satisfied with / happy with…
- ★ I am hooked on / obsessed with / addicted to / passionate about…
- ★ I've developed a great liking for…
- ★ … has grown on me.
- ★ I can't live without…
- ★ I hate / don't like / dislike…
- ★ … is disgusting.
- ★ I can't stand…

Facebook is an online social networking service. After registering, users can create a user profile, add other users as "friends", exchange messages, post status updates and photos, share videos, and receive notifications when others update their profiles. In addition, users can join user groups of common interest organized by workplace, school or college, or other characteristics, and categorize their friends into lists such as "People from Work" or "Close Friends".

Task Work in groups. One plays the role of "Facebook" in order to realize instant communication between the other students. And then the "Facebook" has to outline what they've talked about.

Exercises

Task 1 After you watch the video, what do you know about e-commerce?

Task 2 Discuss with your classmates the advantages and disadvantages of e-commerce.

Unit Six
House Prices

After studying this unit, you should be able to:

❶ understand the background to house prices in China and other countries;

❷ know how to grasp the main idea while you are listening;

❸ know how to use symbols and acronyms when listening;

❹ express opinions point by point.

Part 1 Background Information

    In the decade after 2008, China's property market went through an even more turbulent period than the one in the previous decade. The boom that pumped energy into the economy also created pitfalls. A decade later, economic growth has slowed, the demographic dividend is fading, and high house prices are putting a heavy burden on ordinary families.

House price, a serious issue, is rising though few times of fluctuation in China. The gap between first-tier, second-tier and third-tier cities is widening. Not only in China, people all over the world are experiencing a trend of higher house prices that are putting pressure on their lives.

2008年后的十年,中国的房地产市场经历了一段沸腾岁月,其势头比前十年有过之而无不及,而这种繁荣在给中国经济注入强劲动力的同时,也埋下了隐患。十年后,经济增速放缓,人口红利正在消失,高昂的房价让普通家庭背上沉重的包袱。

房价是一个严肃的主题,中国的房价尽管呈现波动趋势,但总体来说,仍然持续攀升。中国二、三线城市与一线城市的房价差距越来越大。不仅中国如此,世界各地的房价都在不断上涨,这无疑给人们的生活平添压力。

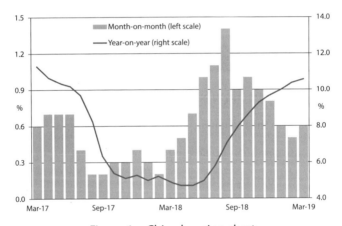

Figure 1　China housing chart

Figure 2　Average house price, UK

Questions

1. Look at the statistics above and compare the housing prices between China and the UK. What are your findings?
2. Discuss with your partner the house price trend in China.
3. What about the house price change in the UK from 2008 to 2010? Work in groups to find possible reasons for the change.

Part 2 Listening Skills

Grasping the Main Idea

There is no doubt that you will always come across some words that hinder your understanding of the whole passage. But if you focus on certain new words, you will definitely lose the whole meaning of the passage as the speaker keeps moving on. A good way to solve this problem is to focus on the words you do understand and the whole context, but not on the words you don't understand. In this section, you will learn how to understand the main idea of certain listening materials and how to guess the words you don't know. You can usually guess the meaning using definition clues, example clues, and contrast clues.

- Definition clues

  Signal words: *be, mean, refer to, be defined as, be known as, be thought of as, be seen as, be regarded as, be described as,* etc.

- Example clues

  Signal words: *such as, including, for example, for instance, to illustrate,* etc.

- Contrast clues

  Signal words: *unlike, dislike, be different from, differ from, but, while, whereas, however, nevertheless, although, even though, despite, on the other hand, like, similarly, similar to,* etc.

Task 1 Listen to the recording and fill in the blanks.

❶ Supporters of the opposition _____ were in a celebratory mood as they anticipated winning most votes.

❷ However, _____ of the seats in parliament are reserved for the _____.

❸ But she did give the statement beforehand that she would not accept _____ in the presidency.

❹ The World Bank has warned that 100 million more people could be pushed into poverty by 2030 unless action is taken to prevent _____.

❺ The World Bank says that climate change is already having an effect on the poorest people who are struggling to raise crops in _____ and _____.

Using Symbols and Acronyms

How can I reduce note-taking time? Taking notes while listening can be difficult. If you take notes word by word, you are likely to lose the main idea of what you are listening to because the speaker is always talking faster than you. On the other hand, if you do not take notes, you may forget some important points after listening. You need a balance. Some listening skills may be necessary while listening, which will help you identify the key points to understand the context and reduce the time spent taking notes.

- Replace words with acronyms and symbols.

To take good notes while listening, you need to write very quickly. At the same time, you need to understand what you are hearing as a whole. But one cannot do two things at one time. Thus, one way to save time is to replace long and complex words with their acronyms. For instance, replace the word "standard" with "STD". Another example is to replace "and" with "&".

- Add notes during a time gap.

You have little time to take notes while listening and you must write quickly, so your notes may be incoherent. A good way to improve is to take full advantage of the time gap between two sentence clusters to make your notes easier to read and understand. For example, you can make more use of numbers and arrows.

Task 2 Listen to the passage and write down the key words. You may use acronyms if necessary to help you understand the main idea of the passage.

_____

_____

_____

Part 1 Intensive Listening

Word Bank

starry *adj.* abounding with or resembling stars 布满星星的，星光闪耀的

unscathed *adj.* wholly unharmed 未受伤的

nag *v.* to bother persistently with trivial complaints 唠叨；使烦恼

collateral *adj.* connected with something else, but in addition to it and less important 附属的；附带的，附加的

JPMorgan Chase an American multinational banking and financial services holding company headquartered in New York City 摩根大通

Task 1 Listen to the recording. Choose T for true or F for false, and then correct the false statement(s).

① Canada's reputation for financial regulation is good. T F

___

② According to Wall Street, a rating agency, Royal Bank of Canada sits alongside HSBC and JPMorgan Chase in the top tier of global banks. T F

___

③ Repeated efforts by policymakers to take the heat out of housing have had no discernible effect. T F

___

④ The maximum amortization period for a mortgage will now be 25 years, down from 30. T F

___

Task 2 Listen to the recording again and choose the correct answers.

① What is the main theme of this passage?
   A. The housing market in Canada.
   B. Some big companies in the housing market.
   C. Canadian policymakers are old hands at pulling the "macro-prudential" levers that are now popular among rich-world central banks.
   D. The differences of the housing market between China and Canada.

② Which of the following hasn't been taken by the finance minister?
   A. Buyers of homes worth more than $1 million have been able to obtain mortgage-default insurance from CMHC with only a 5% down payment.
   B. The maximum amortization period for a mortgage will now be 25 years, down from 30.
   C. Refinancing a home will only be allowed up to 80% of its value, down from 85%.
   D. About a 1% increase in mortgage rates for homebuyers.

Unit Six House Prices

Task 3 Listen to the passage again and fill in the blanks.

Canada's (1) _____ for financial regulation is (2) _____. Its banks got through the (3) _____ unscathed. According to Moody's, a rating agency, Royal Bank of Canada sits alongside HSBC and JPMorgan Chase in the top tier of global banks. And Canadian policymakers are old hands at pulling " (4) _____ " levers of the sort now in vogue among rich-world central banks.

Repeated efforts by (5) _____ to take the heat out of housing have not had a (6) _____ effect. So on June 21st, Jim Flaherty, the finance minister, had another go, his fourth in four years. Some of the new measures were (7) _____. Buyers of homes worth more than 1 million dollars have been able to get mortgage-default (8) _____ from CMHC with a (9) _____ of only 5%. In practice, it is hard to find buyers in this bracket who do not have lots of (10) _____ in their homes.

Part 2 Video-watching

Word Bank

decline *v.* to change toward something smaller or lower 下降

slight *adj.* very small in degree 轻微的

calculation *n.* the procedure of calculating; determining something by mathematical or logical methods 计算，估算

reluctant *adj.* unwilling to do something contrary to your enthusiasm 不情愿的，勉强的

prudent *adj.* careful and sensible; marked by sound judgment 谨慎的；节俭的

Task 1 Watch the video and answer the questions.

❶ What is the whole situation in China's housing market?

_____

_____

❷ What are the improvements mentioned in the video about China's housing market?

Task 2 Watch the video again. Take notes and make an outline. Then, retell it.

Part ❶ Individual Speaking

Word Bank

reanimation *n.* refreshment, inspiration 复活；鼓励

resuscitate *v.* to revive, resurrect 使复苏

flop *v.* to slump, fail, washout, collapse 失败

tantalize *v.* to make a person or an animal want something that they cannot have or do 逗弄，逗引

odd *adj.* strange, queer 奇怪的

Goldman Sachs an American multinational investment banking firm that engages in global investment banking, securities, investment management, and other financial services primarily with institutional clients 高盛投资银行

snap up to buy it quickly 抢购

delinquent *adj.* having failed to pay money that is owed 拖欠债务的

Federal Reserve the central banking system of the United States 美联储

Unit Six House Prices

Task 1 Brainstorm reasons for the rise in house prices.

Reason A: _____

Reason B: _____

Reason C: _____

Task 2 Listen to the recording and answer the questions.

1. What does the passage mainly talk about?

   _____

   _____

2. Why is America's housing finance system as frail as ever?

   _____

   _____

Part 2 Role-play

Task 1 China's house prices have risen sharply in recent years, which has undoubtedly had a significant impact on people's lives. Work with your partner and discuss the following questions.

1. What are the reasons for the rise in China's house prices?

2. How does it affect people's lives?

3. Do you think house prices will be lower or higher in the future? Why?

4. Who will benefit from rising house prices? Why?

Part 3 Group Work

Tips

Useful expressions for expressing viewpoints

- As for me, I am on the latter part of the argument. The reasons are as follows.
- First of all, ...
- Secondly / in the second place, ...
- next/then...
- Thirdly...
- Last but not least / finally / in the end...
- As long as...
- Only in this way...
- I sincerely believe that...

Task Work in groups to share your views on the development of house prices in China. You can use the expressions above to organize your idea.

Exercises

Task 1 Watch the video, and try to write down the key words of this news.

_____

_____

_____

Task 2 What other reasons do you think would make it less expensive to rent a house, but more expensive to buy one?

Unit Seven
The RMB and the SDR

After studying this unit, you should be able to:

① understand the benefits and significance of the inclusion of RMB in the SDR (Special Drawing Rights) basket;

② learn how to make inferences in financial listening;

③ understand how to distinguish between facts and opinions when listening;

④ make comments after listening.

Part ① Background Information

Created by the International Monetary Fund in the 1960s to meet the world's demand for reserve assets, SDRs play a crucial role in the global financial system. Technically, they constitute an international reserve asset that helps maintain a balance between countries with large foreign liabilities and those flush with cash. China always eagers to let the RMB go global and has put the SDR in the spotlight. The Chinese RMB officially joined the SDR basket in 2016. The International Monetary Fund, which manages the SDR, conducted a five-year review of the basket of currencies that make up its value in 2022.

20世纪60年代，国际货币基金组织为了全球储备资产的需要，创设了特别提款权（SDR），在全球金融系统中起到了至关重要的作用。技术上，特别提款权组成了国际储备资产，以保持对外负债多的国家和现金富裕的国家之间的平衡。中国一直致力于人民币的全球化，十分重视特别提款权。2016年，人民币正式纳入SDR货币篮子。2022年，国际货币基金组织进行了每五年一次的SDR货币篮子评估。

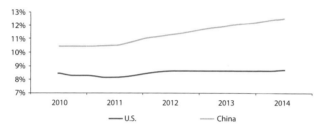

Figure 1　U.S. and China—Share of world exports

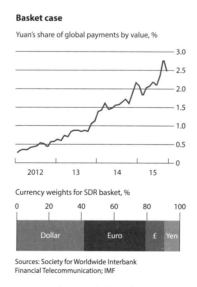

Figure 2　Yuan's share of global payments by value

Unit Seven The RMB and the SDR

Questions

1. Which currencies have been included in the SDR up until now?
2. What is the significance of the RMB's increasing share in global payments?
3. What are the benefits of China's rising proportion of world exports?

Part 2 Listening Skills

Making Inferences

The ability to make inferences, which is often used in reading, also plays a crucial role in improving listening performance. When listening to financial news, do not ignore the information available. Try to use the background information and your own experience to make inferences.

Task 1 Listen to the passage and choose the correct answers.

1. According to the passage, why is the inclusion of the RMB in the SDR basket not a question of "if", but a question of "when"?
   A. Because China is the world's largest exporter.
   B. Because the Chinese authorities are making great efforts to include the yuan in the SDR basket.
   C. Because the RMB is now freely usable.
   D. Because it is quite easy for the RMB to meet the two criteria, but it will take time for the IMF to assess the RMB.

2. According to the passage, which of the following statements is not true?
   A. Christine Lagarde has supported China's efforts to internationalize the Chinese yuan.
   B. The Chinese authorities are well aware of what is desirable and what needs to be

changed and improved in monetary policy and the financial sector in China.

C. China's moves to deepen financial market reforms and liberalize interest rates will certainly not benefit the currency at the review.

D. The European members of the Group of Seven major industrialized economies favor the inclusion of the yuan in the SDR basket before the end of the year.

Task 2 Listen to the passage again and write down the key points according to what you have heard.

_____

_____

_____

Distinguishing Facts from Opinions

Distinguishing between facts and opinions can help you achieve a deeper level of understanding of the material you are listening to. Facts are statements that say what happens or what the case is, and they are usually based on direct evidence. Therefore, a fact can be proved or disproved with direct evidence. Opinions, on the other hand, are not reliable sources of information; they are statements of belief, judgment, or feeling and should be questioned and carefully evaluated. Usually, opinions involve a person's tastes and preferences and show his or her attitude toward a subject or issue. Below are some specific words that serve as clues to opinions.

- Phrases: *I believe..., I think..., I suggest..., in my opinion..., it appears..., it would seem..., one explanation is apparently..., ... is considered to be...,* etc.
- Adverbs: *probably, possibly, perhaps, seemingly,* etc.
- Emotive response (the use of exaggerated or emotional words): *horrified, shocked, unbelievably,* etc.

Unit Seven The RMB and the SDR

Task 3 Listen to the news report and write down what you think are facts or opinions.

_____

_____

_____

Task 4 Listen to the news report again. Based on the facts and opinions you have written down, what's your attitude toward these opinions? Do you agree or disagree with them? Why?

Part 1 Intensive Listening

> **Word Bank**
>
> **International Monetary Fund (IMF)** an international organization of 190 countries and regions working to foster global monetary cooperation, secure financial stability, promote high employment and sustainable economic growth, and reduce poverty around the world 国际货币基金组织
>
> **eligible** *adj.* fulfilling the necessary conditions 合格的
>
> **conducive** *adj.* likely to produce, helping 有助于的
>
> **replenish** *v.* to fill or make complete again 补充
>
> **convertibility** *n.* the quality of being exchangeable 可兑换
>
> **composition** *n.* the combining of district parts or elements to form a whole 组成，构成

Task 1 Listen to the passage. Choose T for true or F for false, and then correct the false statement(s).

1. There are two criteria for assessing if a currency could be included into the SDR.   T   F

   _____

2. China's deepening financial market is helpful for the assessment.   T   F

   _____

3. The SDR basket consists of four currencies: the U.S. dollar, euro, pound, and yen.   T   F

   _____

4. If approved, the yuan would be the first market currency to join the SDR.   T   F

   _____

5. The passage is about the IMF's assessment of when to include the yuan into the SDR.   T   F

   _____

Task 2 Listen to the passage again and choose the correct answers.

1. Which factor is not conducive to an assessment of whether the RMB is freely usable?
   A. The liberalization of interest rates.
   B. Opening up of the capital account.
   C. The export capacity.
   D. Deepening of financial markets.

2. Chinese Premier Li Keqiang asked Lagarde to include the yuan in its SDR basket, pledging to _____.
   A. benefit China's economic growth

B. increase China's GDP

C. promote China's economic stability

D. boost the RMB's basic convertibility

3 According to the news, which of the following statements is not true?

A. Freely usable currency and the export capacity are the two criteria determining whether the yuan can be included into the SDR.

B. There are some people who doubt whether China fits the bill on the export capacity.

C. The SDR is an international reserve asset created by the IMF in 1969.

D. The IMF's board will hold an initial discussion on China's request next month.

Task 3 Listen to the passage again and fill in the blanks.

The assessment of a currency's eligibility to be added into the SDR is based on the two criteria, one is the (1) _____ of the country where the currency is being issued and the other is the (2) _____ as an international currency.

Christine Lagarde, IMF Managing Director, believes that what the Chinese authorities indicated in terms of (3) _____, in terms of (4) _____, in terms of (5) _____, actually will naturally be conducive to an assessment of whether the RMB is (6) _____, which is one of the key criteria. However, as for the other one criteria, the export capacity, nobody doubts whether or not China fits the bill.

Last month, Chinese Premier Li Keqiang asked Lagarde to include the yuan in its SDR basket, pledging to speed up the RMB's (7) _____. The IMF's board will hold (8) _____ on China's request next month. It will also conduct a full five-yearly review of (9) _____ later in the year before making a final decision in November. If approved, the yuan would be the first (10) _____ to join the SDR.

Part 2 Video-watching

Word Bank

Special Drawing Rights (SDR) supplementary foreign exchange reserve assets and maintained by the IMF. Their value is based on a basket key of international currencies reviewed by the IMF every five years. 特别提款权

strategic *adj.* important or essential in relation to a plan of action 战略性的

sovereign *adj.* (of a country) independent and self-governing（国家）独立自主的

swap line another term for a temporary reciprocal currency arrangement between central banks（货币）互换额度

Asian Infrastructure Investment Bank (AIIB) initiated by the government of China, a proposed international financial institution which is focused on supporting infrastructure construction in the Asia-Pacific region 亚洲基础设施投资银行

Task 1 Watch the video and answer the questions.

① What has China done to have its yuan currency included in the SDR?

② Why do experts say it's important to give China a seat in the SDR?

③ What can you infer from the statement that "now typically an 85 percent vote is required for some of the IMF's toughest decisions. In this case, only a 70 percent vote will be needed to determine the inclusion of China's currency"?

Unit Seven The RMB and the SDR

Task 2 Watch the video again. Take notes and distinguish facts from opinions.

_____

_____

_____

Part 1 Individual Speaking

Word Bank

undertake *v.* to take up or accept (a duty or piece of work) 从事
recognition *n.* the state of being accepted as legal or real 认可
associate with to link something in the mind with something else 联合；使联系
exclusive *adj.* limited to one organization, not shared with others 独有的
foreign exchange reserve assets held by a central bank or other monetary authority, usually in various reserve currencies 外汇储备

Task 1 Brainstorm the benefits of including the RMB into the SDR basket.

　　As a major currency for world trade and investment, the RMB accounts for a growing share of international financial transactions and reserve holdings. In 2016, the IMF officially included the RMB in the SDR basket. How does this benefit China, the IMF and indeed the whole world?

　　Benefits for China: _____

　　Benefits for the IMF: _____

83

Benefits for the world: _____

Task 2 Watch the video and answer the questions.

❶ What does SDR mean exactly? And how significant is China's inclusion into the SDR?

_____

_____

❷ What are the economic benefits for China regarding the yuan's inclusion into the SDR?

_____

_____

Part 2 Role-play

The International Monetary Fund has added China's yuan to its benchmark currency basket, a victory for Beijing's campaign to be recognized as a global economic power. But how do you know about China's push to get the yuan into the IMF's elite currency basket?

Task Do a mock interview with your partner. One of you will be the reporter and the other the Chinese official. The following questions may be included in your interview.

- What is the special drawing rights system? Is the SDR a currency?
- Why does China want this status?
- Why does the IMF's assessment of the yuan's inclusion into the SDR take so long?
- Why is the IMF willing to approve of the Chinese currency's inclusion into the SDR?
- What does the official inclusion of the Chinese currency into the SDR mean for the Chinese authorities?

Part 3 Group Work

It has been found that people often have different views on a certain issue. Therefore, how you make comments is very important, and will help improve your critical thinking skills. Here are some tips to help you make appropriate comments.

Tips

- ★ Never leave short and meaningless comments.

  Showing appreciation in some way is nice, but unfortunately short and meaningless comments rarely get noticed.

- ★ Expand the topic.

  If the topic happens to be within your area of expertise, try leaving a comment that expands on the topic. Explore other possibilities and ideas. Think of it as writing a little follow-up.

- ★ Provide personal insight.

  Share your personal experience. Different tips will have different effects on different readers. Sharing your personal experience will help readers identify your situation and anticipate future effects.

- ★ Be communicative.

  Commenting is a form of interaction. Whether you're engaging in a discussion with the author or with the community, it's a good strategy for getting noticed. People often appreciate those who help start and develop interesting and intense discussions.

- ★ Be a critic, not a hater.

  No commentator has the absolute truth. Therefore, he or she must be prepared to be criticized. If you're going to leave a negative comment, try to make credible arguments. Others may accept your views and even be grateful.

Exercise 1

Task 1 Watch the video. Write down the significance of the inclusion of the RMB into the SDR basket.

_____

_____

_____

Task 2 Watch the video again. Create an outline about the experts' opinions. Do you agree or disagree? Why?

_____

_____

_____

Exercise 2

Task 1 Watch the video and fill in the blanks.

❶ _____ has taken 20 years.

❷ In 1996, the Chinese yuan was only _____ its foreign trade destinations, while its _____ remained closed.

Unit Seven The RMB and the SDR

❸ One year after during the Asian Financial Crisis, China conducted _____, and fixed the rate at 8.28 per dollar.

❹ In 2005, China _____. This was the start of RMB's exchange rate mechanism reform.

❺ On July 21, 2015, yuan _____ against dollar after revaluation, and it has adopted a managed floating exchange rate regime.

❻ As of October this year, the PBOC has _____ with 33 countries and regions and involved more than 3.3 trillion yuan.

❼ The People's Bank of China _____ this August, in a bid to push the currency toward a more market-oriented reform.

❽ And two months after, the RMB _____ following the US dollar, the sterling and the euro.

Task 2 Watch the video again. Choose T for true or F for false, and then correct the false statement(s).

❶ The move that China conducted a dollar-pegged exchange rate system was applauded globally because the RMB did depreciate itself to boost exports at that time. T F

_____

❷ Since its inclusion in the SDR, the RMB has practically taken the role of foreign reserves. T F

_____

❸ Foreign central banks hold more than 70 billion RMB, much more than the 10.9% weighting in the SDR basket. T F

_____

Task 3 Watch the video again and write a summary of the video.

_____

_____

_____

Task 4 Discuss with your partner whether Chinese currency's inclusion into the SDR basket can benefit and further internationalize the RMB.

Unit Eight
Consumption

After studying this unit, you should be able to:

❶ understand the definition of consumption and luxury consumption in China;

❷ locate the information you need in business conversations;

❸ know how to use synonyms and paraphrase while listening;

❹ know how to make persuasions in business conversations.

Part ❶ Background Information

Consumption is an important and final link in the process of social reproduction. It refers to the process of using social products to satisfy people's various needs. Consumption is divided into production consumption and personal consumption. The former refers to the use and consumption of means of production and living labor in the process of material production. The latter refers to the behavior and process by which people use the produced material and spiritual products produced to satisfy the needs of personal life, which performs the life function besides the production process. It is an essential condition for the restoration of people's labor and labor production.

消费是社会再生产过程中的一个重要环节，也是最终环节。它是指利用社会产品来满足人们各种需要的过程。消费又分为生产消费和个人消费。前者指物质资料生产过程中的生产资料和生活劳动的使用和消耗。后者是指人们把生产出来的物质资料和精神产品用于满足个人生活需要的行为和过程，是生产过程以外执行生活职能。它是恢复人们劳动力和劳动力再生产必不可少的条件。

Questions

❶ Do you know which corporations make the highest profit?
❷ Can you find out why Chinese consumers are buying more luxury goods from overseas?

Part 2 Listening Skills

Listening for Required Information

A long piece of listening material can make a listener tired or distracted. For some listening materials, only a short part needs to be paid attention to, as the rest of the part may only serve as an introduction or background. Therefore, listeners should have the ability to listen for necessary information, which means that listeners should have knowledge about the topic of the listening material and pay attention to the important parts of the whole material. In other words, listeners should be able to decide which part contains the most important required information and predict what the answers might be.

Before each recording is played, you will have a short time to read the question. Try to predict what the answers might be. This will focus your mind on what to look for in the recording. Occasionally, you'll be able to predict the actual word, but most of the time you'll be able to predict one or more of these three things:

- The type of information needed, e.g., surname, place name, date, phone number, zip code, price, etc.
- The type of word needed, e.g., noun, adjective, verb, etc.
- Synonyms or paraphrases that might be used, e.g., "a quarter" for "25%", "business functions" for "corporate events", etc.

Task 1 Listen to the news. Choose T for true and F for false, and then correct the false statement(s).

1. Companies selling luxury goods gained little from China's economic growth.
                                                                   T   F

   _____

2. A report by the Fortune Character Institute states that China is the world's second biggest consumer of luxury goods.   T   F

   _____

3. Sales of luxury goods have been hit by China's anti-corruption campaign.   T   F

   _____

4. Chinese consumers purchased 76% of their luxury goods while they were abroad.
                                                                    T   F

   _____

5. In China, the markets for luxury goods are dominated by foreign players.   T   F

   _____

Task 2 Listen to the news again and write down its main idea.

_____

_____

_____

Identifying Specific Details

It is recommended that you write down and learn a few common synonyms for each new word you learn. This will help you quickly build up a large and versatile vocabulary. One of the best ways to practice recognizing and using synonyms and paraphrasing is to listen to short videos or podcasts.

This should already be part of your listening test preparation but add this exercise. Every now and then, stop the recording after a single sentence and think about how you could paraphrase it and what synonyms you could use. Do this for a few sentences each day and you'll soon see a real improvement in your listening skills.

Task 3 Listen to the news report. Write down key words and your findings about luxury cars.

_____

_____

_____

Task 4 Listen to the news report again and answer the questions.

➊ According to Dieter Zetsche, what is the capacity of the new engine plant?

_____

_____

Unit Eight Consumption

❷ Why do Chinese people appreciate cars so much?

 Listen

Part ❶ Intensive Listening

Word Bank

Hilton Worldwide a large world hotel company 希尔顿酒店集团

Waldorf Astoria a famous luxury hotel in New York city, managed by Hilton Worldwide 华尔道夫酒店

estimate *v.* to roughly calculate or judge the value, number, quantity, or extent of something 估计；估算

real property property consisting of land or buildings 不动产

raw *adj.* not processed for use 生的；未加工的

security *n.* a certificate attesting credit, the ownership 证券

Sheikhdom the area ruled by a sheikh of stocks or bonds, or the right to ownership connected with tradable derivatives 酋长国

Task ❶ Listen to the recording and answer the questions.

❶ Why did Hilton Worldwide sell Waldorf Astoria?

❷ What industries did the Chinese invest in?

❸ What's the advantage of investing in treasury securities?

Task 2 Listen to the recording again. Take notes and make an outline. Then, retell the report.

Part 2 Video-watching

Word Bank

occasional *adj.* occurring, appearing, or done infrequently and irregularly 偶然的

tuck *v.* to push, fold, or turn (the edges or ends of something, especially a garment or bedclothes) so as to hide or secure them 塞

discount *n.* a percentage deducted from the face value of a bill of exchange or promissory note when it changes hands before the due date 打折；折扣

bargain *n.* an agreement between two or more people or groups as to what each will do for the other 协议；交易

recession *n.* a period of temporary economic decline during which trade and industrial activity are reduced, generally identified by a fall in GDP in two successive quarters（经济）衰退

Task 1 Watch the video. Write down the key words and phrases about this passage.

_____

_____

_____

Task 2 Watch the video again. Choose T for true or F for false, and then correct the false statement(s).

① Consumption is the value of goods and services bought by people. T   F

_____

② Consumption is only a small component of GDP. T   F

_____

③ People with different positions in respect to income have systematically the same structures of consumption. T   F

_____

④ In any condition, the rich have both higher levels of consumption and savings. T   F

_____

⑤ For the consumer, both old and new goods provide some need satisfaction. T   F

_____

Part 1 Individual Speaking

Word Bank

flock *v.* to go or gather together somewhere in large number 涌入

upcoming *adj.* going to happen soon 即将到来的

director *n.* one of a group of senior managers who run a company 高级经理

opposed *adj.* very different from sth. 反对的；不同的

multiple *adj.* many in number 多样的

Task 1 Brainstorm the strategies for dressing appropriately.

If you are about to participate in a fashion show, what will be your strategies for dressing?

Strategy A: _____

Strategy B: _____

Strategy C: _____

Task 2 Watch the video and answer the questions.

❶ In the interview, according to Jarrad Clark, what will the audience see in Berlin?

_____

_____

❷ What are some reasons that Berlin is suitable for holding the fashion show?

_____

_____

Part ❷ Role-play

While the rest of the world cut back on spending, Chinese consumers bought 47 percent of the world's luxury goods in 2013, according to a report by the Fortune Character Institute. Soon, a famous economist will give a lecture on luxury at your university.

Task Work in pairs to create a conversation. One acts as the famous economist and the other as a student who is curious about the phenomenon mentioned above. The following questions may be included in your conversation.

- What is the reason why Chinese consumers buy almost half of the world's luxury goods?
- Is this phenomenon related to global economic conditions?
- Do you think the Western world, such as France, can benefit from this?

Part ❸ Group Work

Tips

Useful expressions for making persuasions

- ★ It is true that ..., but one vital point is being left out.
- ★ There is a grain of truth in these statements, but they ignore a more important fact.
- ★ Some people say ..., but it does not hold water.
- ★ Many of us have been under the illusion that ...
- ★ A close examination would reveal how ridiculous the statement is.
- ★ It makes no sense to argue for ...
- ★ Too much stress placed on ... may lead to ...
- ★ Such a statement mainly rests on the assumption that ...
- ★ Contrary to what is widely accepted, I maintain that ...

Task The phenomenon of excessive consumption is not uncommon among young people. What do you think is the right concept of consumption? Try to discuss your concept of consumption with your partner.

Exercise 1

Task 1 Watch the video and take notes on key words and phrases.

_____

_____

_____

Task 2 Watch the video again and make an outline based on the notes you have written down.

_____

_____

_____

Exercise 2

Task Discuss with your partners whether you will buy a luxury item. List your viewpoints below.

Yes, I will.	No, I will not.

Unit Nine
Stocks and the Stock Market

After studying this unit, you should be able to:

❶ recognize the advantages and disadvantages of investing in stocks, and risks and precautions in the stock market;

❷ predict the theme and related vocabulary at the pre-listening stage;

❸ know how to combine extensive listening and intensive listening in your listening test;

❹ describe and explain the current situation in the stock market.

Part❶ Background Information

    The stock market is the place where shares of publicly held companies are issued and traded, either through exchanges or over-the-counter markets. Also known as the equity market, the stock market is one of the most vital components of a free-market economy because it provides companies with access to capital in exchange for giving investors a slice of ownership in the company. The stock market makes it possible to grow small initial sums of money into large ones, and to become wealthy  without taking the risk of starting a business or making the sacrifices that often come with a high-paying career. Today, most stock market trades are executed electronically, and even the stocks themselves are almost always held in electronic form rather than as physical certificates.

股票市场是上市公司发行和交易股票的场所，包括交易所市场和场外交易市场两种。股票市场，也称股权市场，是自由市场经济最关键的组成部分之一，因为它为公司提供获得资本的渠道，以换取投资者在公司的一部分所有权。股票市场能够集中大量资金，在不承担创业或高投入风险的情况下获得高额利润。如今，大部分股票市场采取电子交易方式，甚至直接发行电子股票，而不再是有形证书。

Questions

❶ How many terms related to stocks are you familiar with? What are they? Can you explain these terms?

❷ What's behind the current stock market volatility? Work in groups to figure out the factors.

❸ To what extent can stocks influence people's lives positively or negatively? List some examples.

Part 2 Listening Skills

Predicting the Theme and Related Vocabulary in Pre-listening

In general, there are two places to predict the topic of the listening material— the title and the questions. In the first case, it's reasonable to infer the theme from the title; while in the second case, you need first summarize the key point of each question and then combine them into a main line to make the final prediction of the theme. Once you have an idea of the theme, it's much easier to predict relevant vocabulary, and the most recommended skill in this process is word mapping. A word map is a cobweb structure of words with a central idea or keyword in the middle and related words around it. The word map also makes it much easier to memorize words and phrases.

Task 1 Read the following questions carefully and predict the main idea of the conversation. Then, listen to the dialogue and choose the correct answers.

① Where did the conversation probably take place?
  A. During a program.　　　　　B. In a classroom.
  C. At a stock market.　　　　　D. In a zoo.

② What do we learn about Neil?
  A. He is both a good and a rich investor.
  B. He is worried about the price of his shares on the stock market.
  C. He likes animals.
  D. He will spend the afternoon in the zoo.

③ What is the conversation probably about?
  A. How to be rich.
  B. How to know whether the stock market is good or bad for investors.
  C. How animals attack each other.
  D. An appointment to visit the zoo.

❹ Which of the following statements is true?

  A. When the price of shares on the stock market is rising, it's a bear market.

  B. When the price of shares on the stock market is falling, it's a bull market.

  C. Experts call the stock market a bull or bear market because the way these animals attack is similar to the way stock prices rise and fall.

  D. It's easy to know the trend of the stock value, although the stock market is unstable.

Task 2 Listen to the dialogue again and fill in the blanks.

❶ But you have to remember that the stock market can be very _____.

❷ It means the _____ of shares can go down as well as up.

❸ It's a _____ market when the price of shares on the stock market is rising.

❹ And the bear, on the other hand, swipes its paws down, so the shares _____.

❺ It was a bull market which stunned even the most pessimistic analysts. The _____ might be over.

Extensive Listening and Intensive Listening

Extensive listening is a way to quickly grasp a general understanding of the material you are listening to. It involves listening to large amounts of texts where the details, such as the exact word or phrase, are not the main point.

Intensive listening is aimed at gaining specific information, which requires more detailed analysis. Therefore, you should try to understand every sentence and even every single word. Sometimes, you may need to listen to the same material several times to get the exact point.

It's effective to combine extensive listening with intensive listening. Before listening, it's a good idea to write down your predictions about the theme and related words. Extensive listening is usually used the first time you listen to get a rough idea of the material. When you listen for the second time, you can focus on more detailed information such as date, number, place, etc. The final listening (if any) is usually used to check your understanding of the entire listening material.

Task 3 Listen to the passage and write down its main idea.

_____

_____

_____

Task 4 Listen to the passage again and fill in the blanks.

Stock market investment	
How does it work?	· When you buy shares in a company, it means that you actually _____. · As a part owner, you benefit by _____ in the growth of the value of the company. · The company benefits by _____ when your shares and other shares are first sold. These funds are used to _____ the business.
What are the advantages of investing in the stock market?	· Direct investment in the stock market gives you control over _____. · Another attractive feature of stock market investment is _____ when your personal circumstances change. · Stock market investment allows you to _____. · Market investment also allows you to follow _____.

Let's Listen

Part 1 Intensive Listening

Word Bank

volatile *adj.* unstable, likely to change suddenly or unexpectedly 不稳定的

stock index stock market index, a measurement of the value of a section of the stock market 股指，股票（价格）指数

halt *v.* to stop 停止

bank reserve the currency deposits which are not lent out to the banks' clients 银行准备金

devaluation *n.* official lowering of the value of a country's currency within a fixed exchange rate system, by which the monetary authority formally sets a new fixed rate with respect to a foreign reference currency 货币贬值

Task Listen to the passage. Choose T for true or F for false, and then correct the false statement(s).

❶ The NASDAQ was the first fully computerized stock market in which investors traded indirectly.　　　　　　　　　　　　　　　　　　　　　T　　F

___

❷ Individuals who want to trade can have free access to the trading system.　T　　F

___

❸ The NASDAQ only trades high technology stocks.　　　　　　　T　　F

___

❹ When the price of a stock goes up, a day trader is likely to buy shares of that stock. And if it continues to rise, the day trader is likely to sell it.　　T　　F

___

❺ Traders may lose all their money or earn a lot of money on the day trading system.

T　　F

Part ❷ Video-watching

Word Bank

stock market crash a situation in which a stock market experiences a sudden major decline in the prices of its underlying stocks 股市崩盘

economic depression a sustained, long-term downturn in economic activity in one or more economies. It is a more severe downturn than an economic recession, which is a slowdown in economic activities over the course of a normal business cycle. 经济萧条

economic bubble a situation in which asset prices appear to be based on implausible or inconsistent views about the future 经济泡沫

herd mentality or mob mentality, describing how people are influenced by their peers to adopt certain behaviors, follow trends, and/or purchase items 从众心理，羊群效应

fail-safe or fail-secure, a device that, in the event of a specific type of failure, responds in a way that will cause no harm, or at least a minimum amount of harm, to other devices or to personnel 自动防故障装置

spooked *adj.* to be scared, to be nervous 受惊的

trigger *v.* to cause, to make something happen 引起；触发

susceptible *adj.* easy to be influenced 易受影响的

Task ❶ Watch the video and answer the questions.

❶ What will cause the most devastating crashes in the stock market?

❷ How did catastrophic events influence the stock market?

3 What are the new threats to the stock market?

4 What is the HFT? How did the HFT affect the stock market?

5 In what way can the regulatory "circuit breakers" help traders before they make their decisions to purchase and sell?

Task 2 Watch the video and answer the questions.

1 According to the speaker, what are stocks?

2 When did a member of the public can first buy shares of Starbucks?

3 If you own Starbucks shares, what can you get?

❹ What is a key institution for encouraging entrepreneurship?

_____

_____

Task 3 Watch the video again. Choose T for true or F for false, and then correct the false statement(s).

❶ One can only receive the profit directly through a dividend payment.　　T　　F

_____

❷ Selling shares directly raises money to fund big ideas.　　T　　F

_____

❸ IPOs provide a big payoff for founders and venture capitalists who invested their time and money when the firm was just a risky startup.　　T　　F

_____

❹ All the savers will wind up happy.　　T　　F

_____

❺ The stock market can be a safer method of investment than investing through banks.　　T　　F

_____

Part 1 Individual Speaking

Word Bank

go public the IPO (initial public offering) process in which shares of a company usually are sold to institutional investors that in turn, sold to the general public on a securities exchange for the first time 上市

savings account accounts maintained by retail financial institutions that pay interest but cannot be used directly as money in the narrow sense of a medium of exchange 储蓄账户

stockbroker *n.* a regulated professional individual who buys and sells stocks and other securities for clients 证券经纪人；股票经纪人

bond *n.* an instrument of indebtedness of the bond issuer to the holder 债券

CD *n.* certificate of deposit, a time deposit as a financial product sold by banks 定期存单

portfolio *n.* a collection of investments held by an investment company, hedge fund, financial institution or individual 证券投资组合

Task 1 Brainstorm reasons why you invest in the stock market or not.

Suppose you are an investor. Will you invest in the stock market? Why or why not? List as many reasons as possible.

Reason A: _____

Reason B: _____

Reason C: _____

Unit Nine Stocks and the Stock Market

Task 2 Watch the video and answer the questions.

1. How is learning about investing similar to learning to ride a bike?
   _____
   _____

2. What are the ways to make money by investing in a stock?
   _____
   _____

3. How do the stocks work as shown in the video?
   _____
   _____

4. Why do investors keep coming back to the stock market even though it is risky?
   _____
   _____

5. What precautions are mentioned in the video to minimize risk?
   _____
   _____

Part 2 Role-play

Many wealthy people invest in the stock market because of its high profitability, but it is not a safe way to make money as the stock market is volatile beyond expectations.

Task Work in pairs to share opinions on investing in the stock market. You can use the following questions to guide your conversation.

- Will you invest in the stock market? Why or why not?

- What are the advantages and disadvantages of investing in the stock market? Support your arguments with appropriate examples.
- Before investing in the stock market, what preparations do you think an investor should make?
- What are the main factors that influence the price of a stock, as far as you know?
- What other tips do you know about investing in the stock market?

Part 3 Group Work

Tips

Useful expressions for talking about the stock market

- ★ ... extremely profitable / make profit (from price difference)...
- ★ ... make numerous people millionaires just overnight.
- ★ To put all eggs in just one basket, ...
- ★ ... give rise to the unexpected and unaffordable result.
- ★ ... suffer big losses.
- ★ To invest irrationally...
- ★ Buy in / hang on...
- ★ Share prices are rising / keep failing.
- ★ ... prices have suffered their sharpest fall since...
- ★ ... price tumbled/surged more than...
- ★ Collapse in prices...
- ★ Fears over...

Task Look at the picture below. Describe the stock market and explain the current situation of the Chinese stock market with your group members.

Unit Nine Stocks and the Stock Market

Let's Practice

◆ Exercise 1

Task 1 Watch the video and take notes on key words and phrases.

_____

_____

_____

Task 2 Watch the video again, and make a comparison between the stock and the mutual fund based on the notes you have taken.

_____

_____

_____

◆ Exercise 2

Task 1 Watch the video. Make a summary of the different types of risks in the stock market and their individual explanations.

Risk types	Explanations

Continued

Risk types	Explanations

Task 2 Discuss with your partners the strategies for avoiding or minimizing risks in the stock market. Then write down your ideas.

_____

_____

_____

Unit Ten
The Gig Economy

After studying this unit, you should be able to:

① understand the impact of the gig economy on employment and economic development;

② learn synonymous substitutions in the process of listening;

③ know how to use shorthand to outline a topic;

④ describe similarities and differences between things.

 Learn

Part ① Background Information

In a gig economy, temporary, flexible jobs are commonplace, and companies tend to hire independent contractors and freelancers instead of full-time employees. A gig economy undermines the traditional economy of full-time employees who rarely change jobs and instead focus on a lifelong career. A wide variety of positions fall into the category of a gig.

The work can range from driving for Lyft or delivering food to writing code or freelance articles. Adjunct and part-time professors, for example, are contract employees, as opposed to tenure-track or tenured professors. By hiring more adjunct and part-time professors, colleges and universities can cut costs and match professors to their academic needs.

在零工经济中，临时、灵活的工作很常见，公司倾向于雇佣独立承包商和自由职业者，而不是全职员工。零工经济破坏了传统的全职员工经济，这些人很少换工作，而是专注于终身职业。各种各样的职位都属于零工的范畴。他们的工作范围从为 Lyft 开车、送餐到写代码或自由撰稿。例如，兼职教授是合同制员工，而不是终身教授。学院和大学可以通过雇佣更多的兼职教授来削减成本，使教授与学术需求相匹配。

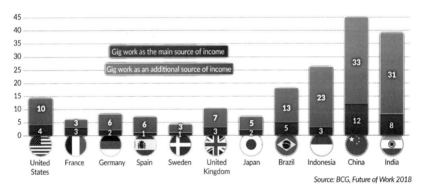

Figure 1　Gig work as the source of income in selected countries in 2018 (%)

Rank	Skill	Hourly pay	Rank	Skill	Hourly pay
1	Intellectual property law	$121.73	11	Book cover design	$32.51
2	Legal consulting	$68.06	12	Financial modeling	$32.46
3	Financial writing	$56.86	13	Corporate taxes	$31.90
4	Voice talent	$56.78	14	Machine learning	$31.84
5	Internet security	$51.39	15	Active directory (programming)	$30.94
6	Language translation	$49.23	16	Infusionsoft development (programming)	$30.85
7	Tableau software	$35.65	17	Microsoft SQL server administration	$30.02
8	Wireless network implementation	$34.86	18	Instructional design	$29.74
9	Industrial design	$34.63	19	Data science	$29.58
10	API documentation	$34.22	20	Cocoa(programming)	$29.50

Source: Upwork

Figure 2　20 highest-paying freelance skills

Unit Ten The Gig Economy

Questions

1. Have you ever heard of the gig economy? Have you ever been a freelancer?
2. Look at the statistics in Figure 1. Why did the gig economy acquire a rapid development in China and India?
3. Look at the statistics in Figure 2. Discuss with your partner what the most important freelance skills are.

Part 2 Listening Skills

Learning to Use Synonymous Substitutions

When you practice listening, you will often find that the information given by the question is not the same as what you heard, but they express the same idea. Recognizing synonymous substitutions, by using different expressions to convey the same meaning, is especially important for improving your listening skills. It is advisable for you to pay attention to the following four types of synonymous substitutions: part of speech conversion, sentence pattern conversion, synonym substitution, and example explanation.

Task 1 This exercise focuses on synonymous substitution. Fill in the blanks after you heard the news report.

1. By 2025, the _____ of the gig economy to the global economy is expected to 2.7 trillion U.S. dollars.
2. Flexible hours, freedom, and control are benefits for _____.
3. Just imagine the benefits for students, the elderly, low-skilled workers and caretakers, but there can be uncertainty like _____, or lack of benefits like _____ or _____.
4. Better _____ products and services are _____ to create financially secure

futures for people in this new gig economy.

❺ We are looking for solutions that can give _____ to gig workers in the domains of spending, saving, _____, or planning.

Task 2 Listen to the news report. Choose T for true or F for false, and then correct the false statement(s).

❶ Drivers and shoppers face the highest risk of the outbreak of virus and also receive the highest protections.　　　　　　　　　　　　　　　　　　T　　F

_____

❷ The risk comes from the random employment.　　　　　　　T　　F

_____

❸ CDC recommendations are good enough to deal with this virus according to some gig workers.　　　　　　　　　　　　　　　　　　　　　　　T　　F

_____

❹ Not just earning profit, American companies also pay attention to their employees' health.　　　　　　　　　　　　　　　　　　　　　　　　　T　　F

_____

❺ Chinese companies' measures have been adopted by gig economy companies here in the US.　　　　　　　　　　　　　　　　　　　　　　　T　　F

_____

Practicing the Method of Shorthand

It is universally acknowledged that when doing listening exercises, it is difficult to record all the key information in the process of listening due to the limited time. A good way to solve this problem is to learn and try to use the method of shorthand, which is a practical technique for recording speech with a special symbol system. In English listening, the two common shorthand methods are abbreviation and symbols. For the abbreviation, there are four main types: removing all vowels (*MKT*: market); keeping the first few letters (*INFO*:

information); keeping the beginning and the end of the sound letter (*WK*: week); writing according to the pronunciation (*R*: are). They can be used to facilitate the note-taking process.

Task 3 Listen to the recording and write down the four ways mentioned by the speaker on how to be a successful freelancer.

_____

_____

_____

Task 4 Listen to the passage again and complete the table according to the information you heard.

	The secret to being a successful freelancer
How to be a successful freelancer?	· What you do. You have to be able to answer the following question: Why would anyone hire you over your _____? Price becomes a _____, and _____ becomes a race to the bottom. · Who you do it for. After you determine what sets you apart, _____ yourself for your ideal customer. · When it's time to talk money, understand the _____ _____ that you create. You're not just being _____ for the time that you work on a project. You're being compensated for everything you've learned and everything you've done over the years that make you _____ at what you do. · Make sure your price includes your taxes, your _____ _____ and your profit. When you're a freelancer, you are your own business, so you're _____ for marketing, accounting, taxes, legal, _____, overhead and profit. If you price too low, you've already _____ against yourself.

Listen

Part 1 Intensive Listening

Word Bank

adaptable *adj.* able to change or be changed in order to deal successfully with new situations 有适应能力的；能适应的

SQL structured query language, a computer programming language used for database management 结构化查询语言

innovation *n.* the introduction of new things, ideas or ways of doing something 创造；创新；改革

collide *v.* to disagree strongly 严重不一致；冲突；抵触

subscribe *v.* to pay an amount of money regularly in order to receive or use something 定期订购（或订阅等）

Task 1 Listen to the news report. Choose T for true or F for false, and then correct the false statement(s).

1. President Vladimir Putin ordered Russian meddling in the 2016 U.S. election to support Donald Trump.   T   F

2. Mike Pompeo said the reliability of this report can't be confirmed.   T   F

3. The 56-50 assembly vote marked a victory for labor unions.   T   F

4. It is easier for companies to classify workers as independent contractors because of this bill.   T   F

Unit Ten The Gig Economy

⑤ The proposal could affect a wide array of industries.   T   F

Task 2 **Listen to the recording and then choose the correct answer.**

❶ What does the passage mainly talk about?
   A. Gig work has replaced traditional work.
   B. Keep learning is important to be competitive in the gig economy.
   C. How to thrive in the gig economy.
   D. There are four good career strategies in a world of short-term engagements.

❷ How can people become adaptable in the gig economy?
   A. Continuous learning.   B. Re-education.
   C. Earning new skills.   D. All the above.

Task 3 **Listen to the passage again and write down the specific words in the following blanks.**

First, train yourself to be _____. At best, this means a solid liberal education and knowledge of the world. Pace of change is _____, and it isn't slowing down. So becoming _____ in your ways can be fatal. You overcome that with a broad base of knowledge, curiosity, and understanding how other people operate.

Second, you need to learn how to _____. Along with that broad base of knowledge, this is one specific skill you'll need to make in the new world. You don't need to become a professional _____, but code is like the _____ of the new economy. And you need to have some grasp of it.

Third, start thinking like a social scientist. The people who make it today can see the big trends early, and add them up to something. So what does that mean for your company or industry? To find something useful out of all of this _____ and data, you need to think like a social scientist. How do people act differently given these trends, and what can I do about it?

Finally, you might want to move to a city. Rapid _____ is the new currency. And this tends to happen more in cities where ideas _____ with each other, and there's a _____ for different ways of thinking.

Part 2 Video-watching

Word Bank

permanent *adj.* lasting for a long time or for all time in the future; existing all the time 永久的；永恒的；长久的

freelance *adj.* earning money by selling your work or services to several different organizations rather than being employed by one particular organization 特约的；自由职业(者)的

sharing economy an economic model defined as a peer-to-peer (P2P) based activity of acquiring, providing, or sharing access to goods and services that is often facilitated by a community-based on-line platform 共享经济

telecommute *v.* to work from home, communicating with your office, customers and others by telephone, email, etc. 家庭办公，远距离工作

Task 1 Watch the video and then answer the following questions.

1. What is the definition of the gig economy?

2. What are the two reasons leading to the development of the gig economy?

3. What strategy does the speaker suggest to deal with the gig economy?

Unit Ten The Gig Economy

Task 2 Take notes and write an outline while watching.

_____

_____

_____

Part 1 Individual Speaking

Word Bank

garment *n.* a piece of clothing; used especially in contexts where you are talking about the manufacture or sale of clothes 衣服（尤用于衣服生产和销售的领域）

shatter *v.* to destroy something completely, especially somebody's feelings, hopes or beliefs（使感情、希望或信念等）粉碎，破灭；被粉碎；被破坏

obliterate *v.* to remove all signs of something, either by destroying or covering it completely 毁掉；覆盖；清除

aphid *n.* a very small insect that is harmful to plants 蚜虫（体小，植物害虫）

aggravate *v.* to make an illness or a bad or unpleasant situation worse 使严重；使恶化

Nordic *adj.* of or connected with the countries of Scandinavia, Finland and Iceland 斯堪的纳维亚的；北欧国家的

emphatic *adj.* expressing something forcibly and clearly 坚决强调的

Task 1 Brainstorming: Recent years have seen the rapid development of the gig economy, especially in some developing countries. Please talk about the reasons behind this rapid growth.

Reason A: _____

Reason B: _____

Reason C: _____

Task 2 Watch the video clip and answer the following questions.

① From the perspective of chronological order, what are the development stages of the gig economy?

_____

_____

② What are the two public policies that can be adopted to make the platform economy a vibrant source of growth?

_____

_____

Part ② Role-play

Unit Ten The Gig Economy

In the "gig economy" or "freelance economy", gig workers earn all or part of their incomes through short-term contracts in which they are paid for individual tasks, assignments, or jobs. By combining multiple tasks for different companies, gig workers can earn cumulative incomes that rival those of traditional full-time jobs. However, in addition to the damage done to traditional work by the gig economy, it also has some drawbacks.

Have a debate on the advantages and disadvantages of the gig economy. You may use the following questions to guide your debate.

1. What are the advantages of the gig economy? Are there any specific examples?
2. What are the disadvantages of the gig economy? Are there any specific examples?
3. Will you choose to be a freelancer after graduation? If yes, what is your priority in making this choice?

Part 3 Group Work

Tips

Useful expressions for describing differences and connections

- When it comes to...
- in comparison with...
- outshine/overshadow
- It's apparent/obvious/self-evident that...
- On the one hand..., on the other hand...
- instead of...
- To some extent...
- On no account can we ignore the importance of...

Task The gig economy is different from traditional odd jobs, but its appearance has something to do with the sharing economy. Please discuss the following three questions and use some specific examples to support your point of view.

❶ What is your understanding of the gig economy, traditional odd jobs, and the sharing economy respectively?

❷ What are the differences between the gig economy and traditional odd jobs?

❸ What are the connections between the gig economy and the sharing economy?

Let's Practice

Exercise 1

Task 1 Watch the video and write down key words and phrases according to your understanding.

_____

_____

_____

Task 2 Watch the video for the second time. Based on the words, expressions and notes you have taken, write an outline about the interview.

_____

_____

_____

Unit Ten The Gig Economy

Task 3 Watch the video again and think about the problems faced by freelancers or independent contractors. What solutions can be adopted to deal with this problem?

✏ Exercise 2

Task 1 This video is about the impact of the COVID-19 on the development of economy, especially the gig economy. Watch the video and answer the following questions.

① What happened to unemployment because of COVID-19?

___

___

② Which companies might collapse?

___

___

③ Will this situation have a political impact?

___

___

④ Will the global economy recover?

___

___

125

Task 2 Will the gig economy have a promising future given the unstable economic situation and some unpredictable factors such as the outbreak of the COVID-19? Discuss with your partner.